BMETR and Self-Management For Students

Decode It For Life-Long Success

About the Author

Dr. M.N. Roy's M.B.B.S degree is from Patna Medical College 1960. He worked in different hospitals in U.K and Eire from 1961 to 1966. He acquired Fellowship of Edinburgh, U.K in 1966.

On his return to India, he worked in Patna Medical College Hospital and later joined Bihar State Health Service and obtained M.S. in General surgery.

He finally settled in the district town of Begusarai servicing the needy masses of the hinterland as a surgeon for over 5 decades.

Dr. M.N. Roy has been credited with many publications in medical journal and has presented numerous scientific papers in State, National and International conferences.

Dr. Roy has also published two books on Management for Doctors.

He has been awarded Fellowship by the Indian Association of Medical Specialties in 1985.

He was presented with a scroll of honour by the Bihar chapter of A.S.I in 2005 for his outstanding services to the society for rendering standard surgical Care and doing Endoscopic & Laparoscopic General and Gynaecological Surgery.

He was elected a Fellow of the Indian Association of Gastro-intestinal Endoscopic Surgeon in 2008.

Dr. M.N. Roy enjoys sports and in his youth represented his college in many outdoor and indoor games. He is a keen & knowledgeable 'rasika' of classical music besides having interest in Indian Philosophy.

Dr. M.N. Roy would be best described by his peers & colleagues as a man of few words but with much to share and impart, an individual of uncompromising integrity, humility and discipline. A healer par excellence, dedicated to the service of the needy, inspiring an ethical and professional   standard for a generation of doctors in the Bihar heartland.

A teacher by example for all those who strive to be the best that they can be.

BMETR and Self-Management For Students

Dr. M.N. Roy, *M.S, F.R.C.S, FIAGES (Laparoscopy)*

To those who are eager to invent a new path for themselves.

ZORBA BOOKS

ZORBA BOOKS

Publishing Services by Zorba Books, July 2020

Website: www.zorbabooks.com
Email: info@zorbabooks.com
Contact: 0124-4259579/8800509579

Print Book ISBN: 978-93-90011-27-8
Ebook ISBN: 978-93-90011-28-5

Zorba Books Pvt. Ltd. (opc)
Sushant Arcade,
Next to Courtyard Marriot,
Sushant Lok 1, Gurgaon – 122009,
India

Preface

I was continuing my surgical practice in a District town of Bihar even a few years back, until, due to some personal reasons, I decided to shift myself lock, stock and barrel to Kolkata. However, being a 70+ stranger here, I failed to establish myself professionally in this city.

This turned out to be an unintended and unplanned retirement with plenty of time and no pastime or work. I found stress, hopelessness and depression staring at my face. To wriggle out of this undesirable quicksand, I took refuge in books and internet. Subjects like lifestyle changes, stress management, physical exercise, yoga, mental fitness and dhyana helped me. I also got attracted to study techniques, memory and brain research. Ultimately, this multi-directional searching and implementing the recommendations therein bailed me out, though gradually. My training in medicine enabled me to comprehend the emerging concepts of the above subjects, including Neuroscience. I was amazed by a few evidence-based emerging facts as mentioned below:

1. Like our grossly visible muscles, memory, IQ, cognitive and emotional faculties are all amenable to training for strength, irrespective of age.

2. A person can alter one's nature and behaviour at will, more so during adolescence.

3. All normal individuals have similar level of memory and intelligence.

4. In study, SQ3R and regular review methods are effective tools. The ancient tools of *shrawan* or listening, *manan* or mulling over and *nididhyasan* or deep meditation are also very helpful.

5. Today, many parents do not have the time or knowledge to guide their wards. They are unable to help them overcome the discomfort of adolescence or mentor them appropriately in academics. The hapless students lacking such family support have to depend on their peers or coaching institutes for it. It often creates stress, thereby, affecting their behavior. Thus, the loud and clear message to such students is to study the matter first, before seeking help from coaching institutes or tutors. The students have to be self-sufficient in other respects too like computer, internet and google search and, of course, taking care of one's BMETR.

It struck me that if these evidence-based concepts are passed on to the students, it will help them in all aspects of their life. Such information did not exist when we were students a few decades back. All this led me to write this book. In fact, I myself had tried these suggested methods mentioned in this book in my late seventies and found them to be quite effective. I was convinced of their benefits.

If followed sincerely, the book will ensure an excellent academic career and will increase a significant chance to crack the tough competitive examinations. It can be a passport to a career of their choice which is what matters the most. Preparing for such examinations require a sturdy dual track of memory and effort on which the carriage of student life will roll on with the help of a 'routine.' The rest of chapters will ensure that the carriage is rendered safe, roadworthy and steady. However, to extract 100 per cent benefit, one has to study the book intensively.

The book also has something for the educationists to ponder upon. The concepts like SQ3R, dhyan,smarana,manana and nididhyasana can be subjects of research. Student volunteer groups can practise these under a 'Double Blind Trial' to evaluate their effectiveness in study and performance in the examination.

Education is incomplete if it ends by giving information only. It has to be understood, lived and researched. The message has to spread to the teaching institutions as well.

Acknowledgement

I am grateful to

Providence which put me in a state of stressful virtual retired life. The same unknown hand which showed me a way out.

Dr. Jitendra Kumar Singh, who encouraged me to write it.

Our extended family members, Shreekant and Mukesh, for the help and guidance that I received from them which sustained me in this effort.

Dr. AsisMukerjee (M.S., F.R.C.S, Mch, Liverpool), an illustrious orthopedic surgeon in Delhi, who is my friend and classmate, and has edited the book with many valuable ideas. I am indebted to him.

Sucheta, my wife; Priyadarshini, my daughter; Agneesh, my son, and his wife, Tulika, for solving the difficulties I faced at various stages in writing this book.

Amit Chakravarty, my brother-in-law, who helped me from beginning till the end while composing this book.

My nephew, Bishwaroop Moitra, who gave me valuable technical advice.

Col. S.R. Chakravortty for his valuable suggestions.

Shri A.K. Bhattacharyya for sharing his experience with me.

Shri RamawtarSultania, industrialist, businessman, philanthropist and my friend, who has rendered invaluable support for which I am so grateful.

Author: Dr. M.N.Roy, July. 2020
E mail: mansuchroy@gmail.com
Copyright: L- 81429/2019

Introduction

Please join me to share the impression of my school days. I was admitted to a school at the age of 10 years in sixth grade around the time India got independence. In those days, guardians had no difficulty in getting their wards admitted in a school. The system was adequate to meet the existing academic standard and demand. We were largely a happy and carefree lot. This has undergone a sea of changes over the past decades. This was a result of increase in population and proliferation of subjects and knowledge. Today, it is an era of competition in education as in other walks of life.

India has the world's largest number of adolescents, between ages 11 and 19. They are over 18 per cent approximately of 1.3 billion of population and are our national asset. You are lucky to be one of them. Such large numbers have resulted in tough contest for a place in a good educational institution. However, you need not worry too much because scientific researches during the last few decades have proved that several measures can help you in cracking tough competitive examinations. At some point of time in school, you have to take a milestone decision about your career and choose subjects accordingly.

The author has coined an acronym by joining the first letters of Body, Mind, Emotion, Time and Routine. BMETR thus represents the basis of our existence, function and self regulation. The body is the hardware, the rest four, its software. Last few decades have seen path-breaking research in various fields. You can take advantage of the emerging concepts which matter most in the following areas:

1. Body (B): Physical exercise have health and other benefits (Dr. J. Morris et al. 1953). Scientific studies have shown that yogahas physical, mental and emotional benefits. (Catherine Woodyard, 2011)

2. Mind (M): Swami Rama's meditation demonstration (In U.S in 1973) has shown that we can increase our mind power to an astonishing level. Meditation seems to improve attention and concentration. (Alice G. Walton, 2015)

3. Emotions (E): Meditation gives us unique control over attention, memory and emotion. (*Sharp Brains Guideto Brain Fitness*, 2013)

4. Time (T): All management methods underline time as a valuable factor to succeed in all spheres of life. Circadian rhythm (sun-based) regulates our body clock and cognitive function. (Conn and Freeman in *Neuroendocrinology in Physiology and Medicine*, 2000)

5. Routine (R): Basically, it is about managing the 24 hours in order to acquire a healthy lifestyle with focus on study and play avoiding useless or harmful worldly distractions. (Thomas Ewer in *The Compelling Science behind Early Morning Starts*, 2015; imgurhttps://imgur.com/7WGa9Bn.jpg)

Last thirty years have also seen advances in study technique. To remember a task longer, SQ3R method (www.niagra.edu/oas) and Mind Map (Buzan 2003) are some of the many tools discussed that will benefit you, as has been discussed in the chapters of this book.

This book is a proposed road map for success in studies and in life. The last three chapters deal with study which forms the most important part of student life. One may ask then why the rest of chapters are there at all? It is because a student faces many distractions and hurdles in everyday life. The rest of the chapters are for managing just that. As a diamond needs to be secured with metal, the act of study has to be kept undisturbed amidst other activities of life.

Since ancient times, parents have been advised to treat 16-year-olds as friends. This liberal attitude will let the children be happy and mature at the same time.

I have written this book from the information gathered from books, internet articles and experiences. I thank the resources to let me share their contribution.

Contents

Contents

1

WHO ARE YOU?

Your Background

Have you wondered why this universe has been created and what is the purpose of your presence in it? While such questions may seem to be difficult to answer, you may find more about yourself readily with daily introspection of your thoughts and activities. You have a visible body in which your mind resides. Mind is the source of both. Besides the Body, Mind and Emotions, we have Time and Routine. Time functions automatically, measured only through a watch or can be roughly guessed with the help of the sun. WE can do nothing to control it. Routine, on the other hand, is fully under our command. I have coined an acronym—BMETR—by joining the first letter of each of the five words (Body, Mind, Emotions, Time, Routine). This book discusses them in detail.

The chapters after this one deal with the assets you have and how powerful your BMETR is. It is like the jinn of Alladin which can give you what you reasonably wish for. These chapters will also tell you what conditions apply which you have to fulfill to get what you want. This chapter is about asking yourself, 'Who are you?'. It is an odd question to ask oneself. If somebody else puts the same question before you, it would perhaps be easier to answer by simply telling your name, address, etc. On the other hand, if you are inquisitive and ask analytical questions— when, why, where, what and how—about your existence, your answers will be different. In fact, you may not even be able to answer some of them now. Please try to find out what you think about the past, present and future. It may be about people, places, ideas, experience or something else. This is your inner world. You are also related to the outer world which you deal with every day. Just calmly see both the worlds during leisure. It can be helpful to be aware of your background. You may learn something about who you actually are.

There is so much fun in observing things. Observation is about what you see with your naked eyes, ask questions and search for answers. You go deeper to draw conclusion about what you have seen. When you observe your inner world similarly by introspection, your questions will find their answers in it and a picture of your background will gradually emerge.

This chapter will be dealing with most of the people and places you will be closely working with and caution you to take care of yourself. Sometimes, perplexing questions may be thrown at you—How this universe with all the flora and animal kingdom including human beings came into existence? What are you going to do in this world? Is it not strange that everyone has a different body, mind and emotional nature?

You may have noticed that there is disparity in families, social and economic background of children living in India. You may find yourself happy and comfortable but have you thought about those who are not lucky as you? There are millions of children who are compelled to waste their childhood in wilderness. Many of them work day and night as bonded labourers, or in shops and industries. They live without proper food and clothing or playtime, away from their family and education.

This dark scenario, however, is no longer as hopeless as before. Nobel laureate, Kailash Satyarthi, has taken an initiative to throw light on such a dark scenario by dedicating his life to their cause and by launching 'BachpanBachaoAndolan' in 1980. The visionary has set up a successful NGO to rehabilitate, educate and reintegrate the downtrodden within our society. He has brought hope to such children. He is also a global pioneer of 'Education for All' concept, especially for underprivileged children. At present you may not be able to do anything to help them. However one should be aware of such uncomfortable realities that exist. May be one day you may be in a position to help them.

The Ramanujan School of Mathematics is another institution that is globally famous as institute of 'Super 30'. It finds 30 meritorious students from the economically backward sections in the country and prepares them regularly for admission test of Indian Institute of Technology (IIT)—India's most prestigious and successful educational institution. The students are provided free coaching, lodging and food. In the last seven years, it has produced hundreds of IITians.In fact, recently, a film has been released, portraying their struggle and success in life. So, there is some hope for such needy students belonging to the lowest strata of the society. There are other organisations too that work for the slum children to have a better life.

Head Office of Home

Your home is the head office of your activities and day's planning. All the members, that make your home, are your own and are well-wishers. They are your source of strength and inspiration to achieve success in life. This mutual bond of love binds you not only till your adulthood but it continues throughout your life. It is natural that you become attached and affectionate to the members of the family. Such a strong bond will give strength and help to enlarge your vision. Your parents not only look after your needs but also share the responsibility to raise you to become a good human being. A teacher gives you knowledge with care and parents provide you everything you need with love. In their attempt to do so, they occasionally happen to restrain you from doing something which always turns out to be for a good reason.

Let me share this anecdote with you—one evening, a crab came out of the sea cheerfully to take a walk on the silvery beach. After a few strides, it looked back to admire its own footprints on sand. They appeared glorious, glowing pink against the rays of the setting sun. Suddenly, a wave from the sea lashed onto the foot prints to erase them in a second. The crab was devastated and complained to the sea who was his best friend, 'Look what you have done! I thought you were my friend and a well-wisher, but I find that you have erased my beautiful marks. Now I have lost faith in you'. The sea then replied, 'I saw some fishermen coming this way and knew that they would trace you from your footprints. They would have caught, culled and eaten you up. So, to protect you, I hurriedly washed away all your footprints'.

Similarly, parents shield you from all odds like an oyster shell. We too respect and care for them in turn, naturally. Thus, a lasting relationship is built between children and their family, since ancient times, Mother, Father and Teacher were revered in that order.

Action Area of School

When your adolescence sets in, you develop an additional identity. The child-like image gradually changes because of physical and mental maturity. You also develop a sense of self-esteem. Now you can do things in ways which you could not earlier. Taking note of this, the family, school, society or friends accept you as a mature individual. It is even possible that they might ask you to share some work and responsibility. This may lead to more work depending upon your capability and cooperation. You gather more experience and esteem. At this point you also have to be careful to safeguard your study time.

You spend 50 per cent of quality time of your life at school (excluding sleeping time). There you gain knowledge, direction and an idea about social life. This is where you get through the minor and major examinations to enter an institution of higher learning or university. To absorb the best from teachers, attention in the class is necessary. It offers an excellent opportunity to learn and make mindful listening a habit. One can learn how to solve difficult problems by asking teachers or seniors even outside class. The ultimate aim is to prepare well to get through the several tests and competitive examinations.

The school is the place to prepare for it. One can learn note and mindmap making, remembering headings, subheadings, keywords and diagrams and tables. To study the chapter taught by a teacher in the class, in library or at home is a great habit. It will pay you in the long run with good results.

If you are well prepared for each of your lessons for the next day, you will automatically have the urge to go to school. School is the place to find out solutions to problematic lessons or grasp concepts you fail to understand. Whenever in doubt, you must ask questions to teachers in the class. It is in school that you are taught to be disciplined, play games and have good manners. It is here that you learn how to thank somebody for doing you a favour.

It does not cost you anything to develop a good relationship, manners and leave a nice impression on people you meet. It is not necessary that you should help only the friends or those whom you know. A helping hand to a needy is always laudable.

I, however, once failed in this unpardonably.

I sailed for United Kingdom and Ireland in 1961 for training and higher studies in surgery. After a few months, I suffered from tuberculosis of lungs in Ireland. The health authorities of that area had arranged for my best possible treatment. The good treatment of doctors and care of the matron and nurses there had cured me. I was given financial support and a six-months-job after I came out of the sanitarium.

During my stay there, my bosses, nurses and friends were kind enough to visit the hospital to encourage me.

Even some of the people of the area, who came to see their relatives and friends admitted there, also came to wish me well. I was eventually cured after 18 long months.

But I curse myself for not meeting the staff of the hospital—who did play a big role in my recovery—after being discharged. Neither did I visit the health authorities to thank them personally. Till date, I carry this guilt of omission because one's conscience does not spare any one. So please avoid such mistakes and accept your failing, and say sorry whenever necessary.

In the school, you pick up the skills to make friends and learn how to behave with others. You come to respect teachers and your seniors.

Some students develop a friendly way to deal with people and peers. They learn the knack to get out of a sticky situation, thus, improving their self-confidence. You can always guess who will extend a helping hand in future and can befriend them, but try to steer clear of people who do not wish well. Generally, it is better to be patient and tactful with senior students. It may keep their fearsome ragging at bay. All these are interpersonal skills which help you in later life too. You can thus grow up as a likable, friendly, noncontroversial person.

Schoolmates (peers) and friends play an important role lifelong. Friendship develops when two or more people have a common interest in studies, games or any other matter. Sharing experiences, learning from each other, in fact, most of our activities can be more enjoyable when shared. Naturally, you spend more time in company of friends than your family as you grow up. It is wise to know early whether a friend is genuine. However, it is difficult to guess whether a friend is genuine or not. With age, time and experience one gets to know it. Avoid taking risks while dealing with friends till you know them well. It is wise to be discreet in taking sides in any dispute between two sides, unless you are confident about the facts.

Be Your Own Security Guard

A student should know that the society has both good and bad elements in it. Your family takes care to keep you away from the bad people. However, as you grow up, your contacts also grow. Your family cannot possibly monitor your safety as before. It, therefore, becomes necessary that you develop ability to discriminate between what is good or bad for you. You learn to avoid bad company or bad habits like smoking or drugs which can ruin your career. You must be careful of this 'Danger Zone.'

Most students are capable of looking after themselves. However, it is wise to be aware of the thugs in the society with their agents operating in schools too. They run drug and sex rackets to extort money from innocent youth, who are an easy and vulnerable prey to such things.

They lure young boys and girls to addiction. At first these criminals supply drugs like Marijuana, Opium, Heroin and other drugs and even alcoholic drinks to the students for free. Within a few days of consuming them, the victims get hooked to the 'feeling good' effect. Soon it compels them to use it daily without which they cannot live. In order to get their supply of the drugs which are costly and not available in market, the helpless youth become dependent on these criminals for its supply. Then the rogues force the victims to objectionable acts and take pictures or videos to blackmail them.

What is worse is to continue with the habit. The addicts who are mostly in their teens, start stealing money to buy intoxicants from them. The victims have to pay heavily in cash and kind and are reduced to physical and mental wrecks. They are too afraid to disclose the truth to their family or friends. They feel isolated and helpless and do not know what to do. Some of the victims may abstain from the habits for a while, but more often than not their poor physical and mental condition prove to be too weak to resist the drugs. Ultimately, they fall back to the bad habits once again.

If, somehow, they muster the courage to tell the truth to the family or police, then there is a chance to come out of this grim situation. The family takes care of the poor victim's physical and mental health by de-addiction treatment and therapy. The police and law can bust the racket and send the culprits behind bars. Such action will save other children in future. This is the correct and wise step to resolve the problem for good. But most victims fail to take this step for lack of courage. They are forced to drop out of school and part with their friends and even their normal ordinary lives. Every family should be eternally vigilant to keep an eye on every ward's activities and well-being. They should be on the lookout for signs of addiction, also termed as Substance Use Disorder (SUD) in him/her(Shahid Ali. Et.al, 2011). The symptoms and signs are—a change in mood, keeping oneself aloof, lethargy and deteriorating performance at school, loss of appetite, weight and worsening temper. There can be less inhibition, lack of motivation, over confidence, trembling, uncoordinated movement, suspicion, slow response, change in behaviour. There can also be increased heart rate, red eyes and dilated pupils. The young ones occasionally come home late, being high on drugs or drinks. They may show injection marks on the front of their elbow. They may skip classes or drop out of schools. They hold a pessimistic view about life and can develop suicidal tendencies. The students should be watched by the parents routinely but with discretion. It should not arouse suspicion in them of being monitored. They may need a specialist doctor's advice.

Appropriate, wise and compassionate steps by parents may prevent the adolescents from taking drugs or can even bring the addicts back to normal. The parents after all are the biggest influence during the formative years of life of pupils universally. This should be conveyed by the parents indirectly during their conversation. The onus is on guardians to set an example by their way of life and habits. The budding students of such homes have been found less prone to drugs and alcohol. The guardian's best investment is to establish mutual love, friendliness and trust. By engaging their young ones in talks and spending time together regularly will ensure stability, security and lasting happiness to such a relationship. The parents can then have a natural authority to ask their sons/daughters directly if they have any such bad habits. The chances are children will confide the truth at least in whom they usually do. Parents know that adolescence is a tough period to endure and should say so to their wards who eagerly wait to hear such encouraging words and regular chats.

Ideally, those parents who are culprit themselves in this respect should apologise to their wards upfront and should be prepared to get back their moral right by giving up such substances for good. Think of the respect one will then earn from their dear ones.

All addictions are harmful. Let us take the example of cigarette—The smoke we inhale actively or passively enter the bloodstream within seven seconds. Even one puff will do some harm. It reaches the blood, brain, lungs, heart and all the body cells. Over there, it releases nicotine, carbon monoxide and hundreds of other toxins. They cause numerous diseases including cancer in the long run. Those who are near the smoker also inhale the toxic smoke and are affected even more. It has been medically proved that all addictions like bidi, paan, supaari (betel leaf and nuts), chewing tobacco, gutka, lime (chuna) and catechu (Katha) can cause cancer and other deadly diseases. The habits of smoking, alcohol and drugs will ruin your health, career, family, stamina and life. It will spoil your good work of many years in a very short time. Many otherwise intelligent but innocent boys and girls are often lured into the trap of such addictions.

The ideal treatment of any disease or problem is its prevention. The best and permanent solution is to resolve not to touch or consume such substances ever. Vow not to use any known object of addiction even once—not even to experiment—or spend time with such addicts. This will keep you out of trouble.

General Tips

You Can Follow to Stay Out of Trouble:

- It is better to avoid people who praise your appearance or intelligence or that of your family members without a legitimate reason to do so.
- It is wise not to make friends with strangers and persons of doubtful character.

- Please discuss all awkward matters with the family first before acting on it.
- Never accept any free gift or offer of free cold or hot drinks or chocolates or sweets from people you do not know well enough.
- Refuse to accept a lift in a car unless you know the person well.
- You have all the resources to solve any problem if only you are observant and use your brains. If necessary, consult your senior or guardian.

An Adolescent in Jungle

A tourist was walking by a rivulet taking photographs with his mobile camera. He saw a herd of wild buffalos running on the other side of the nullah (water body). The tourist was happily capturing the scene on his camera. Soon it was apparent why the buffalos were speeding. A pack of lions were chasing them. A young buffalo, not being able to keep pace with the herd, got down into the rivulet to escape. He had hardly stepped into the water when a waiting crocodile gripped one of the buffalo's legs in his jaws. The stout calf held his ground, resisting its pull with all his might. This prevented the croc from dragging him into the water.

Soon an opportunist lioness claimed her stake by grabbing the thigh of the buffalo. The drag of the croc and the pull of the lioness created a sort of impasse. The three animals now were poised like statues. The tourist was clicking away in delight. The young buffalo, in pain and fright, continued his frantic calls for help. Fortunately, fate favoured the hapless colt at last! The herd, on hearing calf's call, realized that one of them was missing. They returned at once to the spot. Now the balance had changed in favour of the poor calf. The leader of the buffalo herd led the charge against the lions on the bank. The latter, until now, were waiting and watching from a high ground. Seeing the danger of being out numbered, the lions took to their heels. The lioness holding the calf also preferred discretion to valour and shied off.

Delighted to see the herd at his rescue, the calf acquired a newfound strength. With a violent heave, he freed his entrapped leg. In a flash he jumped to safety and disappeared in the retreating herd. He left behind a message though—*never give up*!

Mind Map 1: UNDERSTANDING WHO YOU ARE

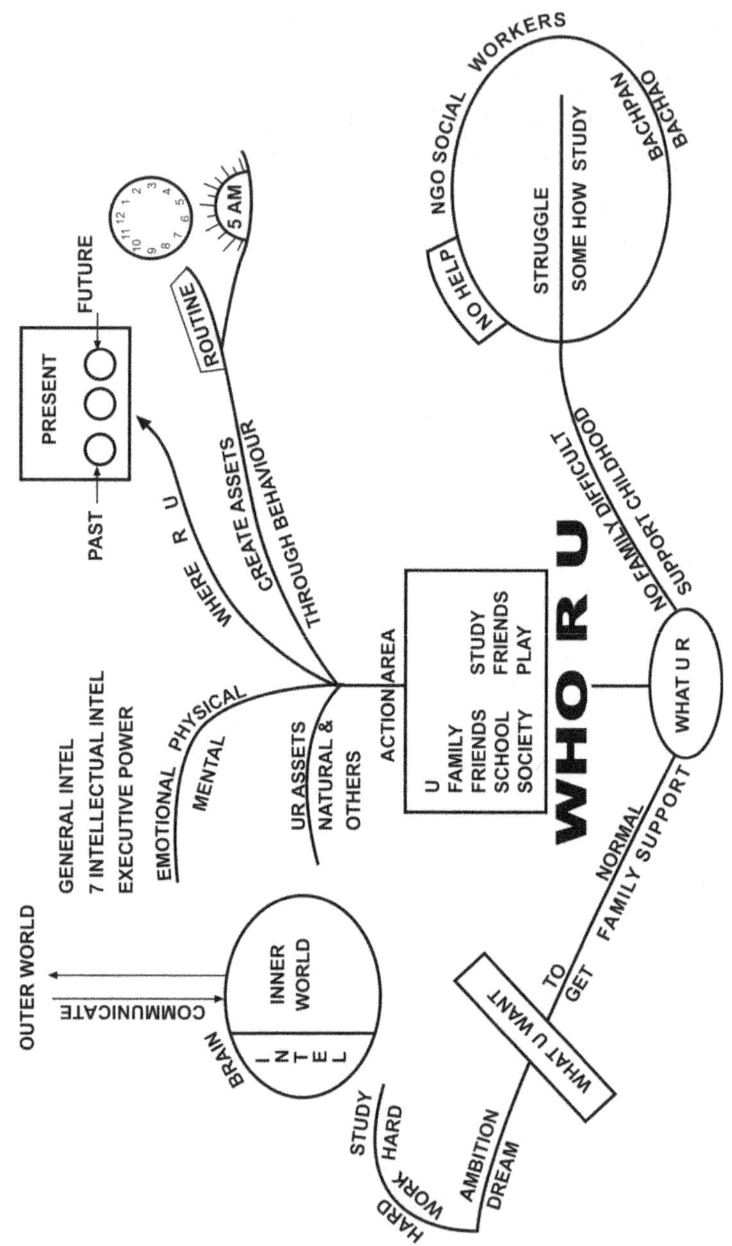

<u>2</u>

YOUR NATURAL RESOURCES

Brain Is Stronger Than Brawn

Till a century back, physical strength was a critical asset for work and life. For ordinary people, it was difficult to earn their livelihood without investing physical labour. In the past hundred years, however, scientific advances have increasingly changed this concept. Now intellectual skill is the key to earn. This is why today most of the students like you at school and colleges aspire for higher education. The various skills in different areas of knowledge, such as super specialisation in medicinelike other branches of science, are in great demand today. Thus, brain now has assumed a place of prime importance over brawn.

BMETR (Body, Mind, Emotion, Time and Routine) is our natural resource and a means to secure our needs. However, like other resources, the body—being the custodian of METR—remains indispensable to us but not for earning a living as much as it was in the past.

It is the brain trained by education that drives our BMETR, to play a dominant role in our life. Today, the thrust of science and technology has shifted more in the domain of brain function, intelligence and their application. This has come about in a big way during the last three decades. Brain is the fountain of all the resources. It seems likely to dominate in future too and, therefore, will be given due importance in this chapter. Even without formal education, we all naturally possess the undermentioned intelligences which can be augmented profitably.

Your Eight General Resources

These are handy tools which need skillful application by repeated use in everyday life. Like our muscles, they can be exercised and made stronger.

1. Inquisitiveness and Imagination: become apparent when we are only a few weeks old. A baby responds to the information they get through their special senses like touch, smell and sound, vision and taste. As we grow older, we increasingly appreciate information we get through our five senses. We, at the same time learn to respond and communicate. We analyse and remember by posing questions (WH-formula). The questions can be who, when, where and which and are closed in nature with answers short and specific. Examples of open ones are how, what and why (www.oakton.edu/learn). The answer in such cases will be descriptive and subjective. Such analytical queries help to acquire memory and insight. Sense of enquiry can be enhanced by adopting an attitude of enquiry, interest, exploration and wonder to every information or object we come across.

I would like to tell you about how inquisitiveness motivated me in my professional life. In 1991, I had gone to Ahmedabad to attend a surgical conference. In one of the sessions, the well-known surgeon, Dr. Tehemton Udwadia, addressed the delegates. The topic was 'Laparoscopic Surgery', which was till then unknown to us. He showed us how to remove the entire gall bladder with stones with the help of three openings of about half an inch long in the abdomen. We were using 5–6 inches long cut in the abdomen. He showed a video of the procedure and answered our doubts and queries. This method was patient-friendly as they could return home in just two days instead of a week as was the norm with traditional surgery. We were all spellbound. I bought a book on the subject written by Dr Udwadia soon after the lecture was over. Later, I attended the first laparoscopic surgery workshop same year in Mumbai.

Now I was eager to learn and perform such surgeries in Begusarai. This was difficult in a district town because of lack of amenities and infrastructure. However, the problems were overcome because I was determined. Initially, I did exploratory operation to sharpen my skills with the new instruments. Then I operated on a dog laparoscopically with anaesthetist, Dr. Anil, along with my assistant colleagues. It was a thrilling experience for all of us. The dog soon recovered fully and took his meal after a few hours. The canine patient however broke his leash after three days and disappeared from the hospital premises without any post-operative instructions! The dog gave us practical knowledge of laparoscopy with a message to keep up the spirit of inquisitiveness. We started doing major laparoscopic surgery at Begusarai in early 1993.

2. ***Knowledge:*** Passing examinations in school and colleges ensure a certain level of knowledge gained by you. One can, however, continue to acquire knowledge beyond the text books. Some people even earn good money in TV serials like *Kaun Banega Crorepati* by sheer hard work to gather general knowledge. Research is going a step beyond knowledge. It is passion, curiosity and imagination to dig out unknown information. Einstein and C.V. Raman became famous for their contribution to science. You too can strive to achieve whatever you like.

3. ***Skills:*** It is an ability acquired by knowledge, training and practise to perform a difficult task efficiently. You are then highly rated in that field. There are super specialist doctors like Urologist, Specialist engineers in metallurgy and Computer science and so on. The physical skills of Jackie Chan have made him a world-famous celebrity actor.Keen and accurate observation is the first step of acquiring any Skill. We pay attention to any particular object, subject, statement, thought, person, concept or a process. At the same time, we note the relevant details such as size, shape, number, colour, movement use and effects about the object under examination. With practise, weget an insight and ability to acquire any skill related to it.

4. ***Motivation:*** It is sustained positive energy and interest to pursue and achieve a goal. Successful people think over what they like to achieve and define the steps necessary to reach it. They write their commitments, read them every day and work hard to execute with a well thought out plan. They also check their progress made from time to time. This is how they keep themselves motivated until the goal is achieved.

5. *Workout:* Practise is the key to become skilled in any area. The degree of competition has become tough because of the increasing number of students. This demand has set a high level of excellence in competitive examinations for success. One has to work hard to learn and be able to reproduce the knowledge verbally or in writing or solving MCQ (multiple choice questions) readily.

6. *Will:* It is the concentrated form of desire. The intensity and consistency of your will determines the extent to which you can exert and cross hurdles. This passion or will sustains your effort to continue for long. It makes you successful in the long run. It was this quality which enabled Mahatma Gandhi to lead India to Independence. All obstacles on his way melted like ice.

7. *Opportunity:* It is a window of Time, Circumstance and Chance. Smart people are always on the lookout for these elements. The credit goes to those who can spot and grab it with both hands first. You are lucky to study in an institution. There are millions of children who cannot afford any education.

8. *Common Sense:* It is a mix of one's general knowledge, intelligence and ability to find a safe and practical solution to a problem. It comes with age, experience and self correction through practical use of general resources.

The seven specific intelligences you possess

It was first classified by Nobel laureate, Gardner H, in 'The Intelligence and its Application' (1983). These intelligences can be enhanced enormously by anybody till any age. You only need a sustained desire to learn and hone it.

- Language: e.g., writer, poet. e.g., Premchand, Mirza Ghalib
- Mathematics: e.g., scientist, computer programmer. e.g., Einstein, C.V. Raman
- Music: e.g., singer, music composer, director and conductor. e.g., S.D. Burman, Lata Mangeshkar
- Spatial (that involves space): e.g., painter, architect. e.g., M.F. Hussain
- Physical Skills: e.g., dancer, gymnast. e.g., Dara Singh
- Interpersonal: e.g., orator, negotiator, executive. e.g., Narendra Modi
- Introspection, changing behaviour, philosopher. e.g., Tulasi Das, J.Krishnamurti

Please note that all these seven categories of intelligences are present in you and me. We all use them every day. They can be improved limitlessly by regular practice. You Also can develop them to a remarkable extent and become a professional in a specific field. Such gifted people become world famous when they create a unique concept by delving deep into any one of the above subjects.

The geniuses like Sachin Tendulkar and Steve Jobs have proved that after all it is not necessary to be proficient in all the intelligences. Mastering even a single skill can make you successful professionally. So, young friends, keep using your BMETR to attain that particular goal which you like most.

The Brain Is an Intelligent Computer

Structure and Function: Human brain is the most evolved among all living beings. Our brain is the initiator, director and controller of all our activities at conscious or unconscious levels. Thus, the brain manages our BMETR totally, that is practically the life itself.

The brain is a unique mass of nervous tissue weighing approximately 1300 gm stored in the safe keeping of the cranium (top of the head). Basically, it deals with sending and receiving information before it decides what to do about them. It is of utmost importance to know about it in details.

The brain has one hundred billion cells called neurons. An individual neuron acts like a computer and also can make ten thousand connections with other neurons. This ability to connect one neuron to the other is called neuroplasticity a word made from Neuron, (functional unit of nervous tissue is neuron and plasticity denotes moulding). Thus, a vast network of connection of information can be created. Special senses pass on information from different parts of the body to specific areas of the brain through such network. The brain in turn responds to these messages by ordering the body parts for appropriate action through its executive network. Neuroplasticity is a lifelong ability to establish new connections with other neurons on which our knowledge and skills depend. The series of exchange of information keeps the BMETR orientation in harmony.

Brain's cognitive functions include thinking, imagination, attention, concentration, cognition (perception), memory, taking decisions, body movements, maintaining balance, ability to analyse oneself, change one's behaviour, etc. The information received by it are recognised and processed, that is, stored (short and long term memory), collated and edited. After processing, a response is sent out in verbal or nonverbal mode. Most of these are within our control and we can operate them at will. For example walking, talking and writing. While some other functions take place involuntarily i.e. without our knowledge like heart beat, digestion and breathing.

There are two parts of brain—right and left. Left is dominant in right-handed persons and vice-versa. Both work together in most actions, but have dominant roles in certain specific field of intellect as mentioned below.

Left brain: Sense of language, logic, calculation

Right brain: Sense of space and distance like painting, architecture, creativity or abstract concepts.

Only 10 per cent of people are left-handed. You too, if right handed can develop your skills with left-hand by appropriate exercise, practice to write or become a better sports person by practicing to bat or bowl with the non-dominant hand.

Exercise of mind by challenging the intellect increases the number of connections of neurons. This network of multiple connections called neuroplasticity is an integral part of learning and other brain functions. It can be made stronger by challenging the mind regularly *(See 'Review' in 'The Way to Study' chapter).* The connection will become weak if you don't use it or challenge your mental faculty regularly. We can apply nature's universal gift of exercise to other members of BMETR also and make them stronger.

The dictum is 'use it or lose It.' Neuroscientists believe that we use only 10 percent to 19 percent of our intelligence. So, our capacity to improve it further is vast.

Self Regulation: The Brain is unique because it can structurally change itself with active intervention. If you want to get rid of bad thoughts or habits or even a certain kind of behaviour, you can do it. However, it requires a strong will supported by appropriate action. In an interview with the authors of *The Sharp Brains Guide to Brain Fitness* (2013), Robert Bilder has discussed how to change behaviour. He has quoted another researcher, Dr. Prochaska, in this connection. Behaviour can be changed in stages. First action (pre- contemplation) is to think regularly to decide what one wants to change. Second, (contemplation) is to meditate about it. Third, act on it or practice it. Lastly, he has to keep practising it for at least six months. This will create a new pattern of behaviour, replacing the old, called reprogramming, by changing the neuronal plasticity and connections.

The Four Brain Waves: It is a recordable electrical activity of the brain. There are mainly four brain waves. One of them, the Alpha wave, is most important for study and memory. Kevin Paul, in his book, *Study Smarter Not Harder* (2013), has lucidly discussed it. Alpha waves change the mind to an alert and relaxed state at the same time. Then the mind can think clearly, understand, introspect, remember and easily solve problems. You feel a flow of energy and confidence within. Athletes too experience such an inspiring state. I am sure you also must have felt it occasionally during study or playtime. During this phase, your performance is excellent. One can get into such a state of mind more often by doing any work mindfully and by meditation.

Delta = Deepsleep, Dhyana; Alpha = study alone, आत्मनिरीक्षण (INTROSPECTION); Beta= बोलचाल (CHATTING); Theta = thoughts, imagination.

How we learn something: We receive information through our five special senses. They are the eyes (visual), ears (audible), nose (olfactory), tongue (taste and a special tactile sense) and skin and mucous membrane (sense of feel or touch). The Brain processes information it gets from these special senses. It then responds through the five executive channels of the body. They are moving, grasping, speaking, elimination and reproduction. These sensations are all recorded in memory which is an integral part of learning. It is through this import and export of information that the business of life is conducted. Individuals can improve one or all of the faculties of BMETR by exercising them intelligently in day to day activities.

Advantages of mental exercise: By challenging the intelligence, related specific areas of the brain grow bigger due to formation of new connection (neuroplasticity). This has been confirmed by Pet scan studies. In an interesting study on London Taxi drivers who have to remember the various roads, streets and lanes it has been seen that due to their frequent recall of these pathways, they develop a thick Hippocampus which is an area of the brain related to memory (*The Sharp Brains Guide to Brain Fitness*, 2013). Such findings have also been detected in medical students during their preparation for important examinations.

You might feel happy and secure by what you have read in this chapter. You may rightly come to believe that nature's gift is a part of human evolution. But there is another side to nature's legacy. We also have mental hurdles like arrogance, laziness, stress, etc. which prevent us to concentrate on the job at hand. The clever ones counter these negative elements by replacing them with a positive awareness and attitude.

How many hours you have toiled is unimportant, what you have achieved in those hours is the real thing.

An incredible story of a student: Through personal communication (courtesy Mr. A.K. Bhattacharya)

An eight-year-old boy was eagerly waiting to touch his newly born baby brother lying in the lap of their mother. When he did, his expression was as if he was pleading, 'Mother, will I not ever be able to see my brother?' It was because the boy was born deaf and dumb. Sometime after his birth, this poor boy had started losing the sight of both his eyes and within a few years he was deaf, dumb and blind. The mother could only grieve silently.

The hapless parents, both school teachers had spent their resources on the boy's treatment earlier in Kolkata and Chennai. Every specialist expressed his inability to help and said, 'Now only God alone can help the boy.' There was no school in India for the 'Deaf and Blind' (as the handicapped were called) at that time.

As the boy grew up, two features distinguished him. One was that the boy was passionate to learn about the world he could not see. The second was that he was restless to do something on his own. He had endless energy to pursue them. He would wait with remarkable patience for the answer he was seeking.

His parents responded with befitting fortitude. They would make the boy familiar about the world which he was largely unaware of. While the father explained, the boy would hold his father's hand and absorb all that he had to say. It may sound strange to us but as is well known, such differently-abled persons develop extraordinary perceptive abilities. By touch alone they are able to grasp many things which normal people cannot. This way, the lad gained a fair amount of knowledge.

As luck would have it, he obtained a US scholarship to study in the famous Perkin School For Deaf Blind, Boston. He went there with his father and never looked back—winning many medals, commendations and certificates during his stay.

He is now well known in his field and is working as a supervisor at the Technology Centre, New York. He is invited to present papers in his specialised field of Computer Research and to teach deaf blind students in different parts of the world. This is done through Braille enabled computer, sign language and special interpreters. This, in short, is a brief introduction of the extraordinary AnindyaBapin Bhattacharya. He has proved that with a passion to know, combined with a will to do something constructive, one can change the impossible to possible. He has been awarded for his contribution in communication for the Handicapped in U.S. and in Chennai recently.

Mind Map 2: KNOW YOUR NATURAL RESOURCES

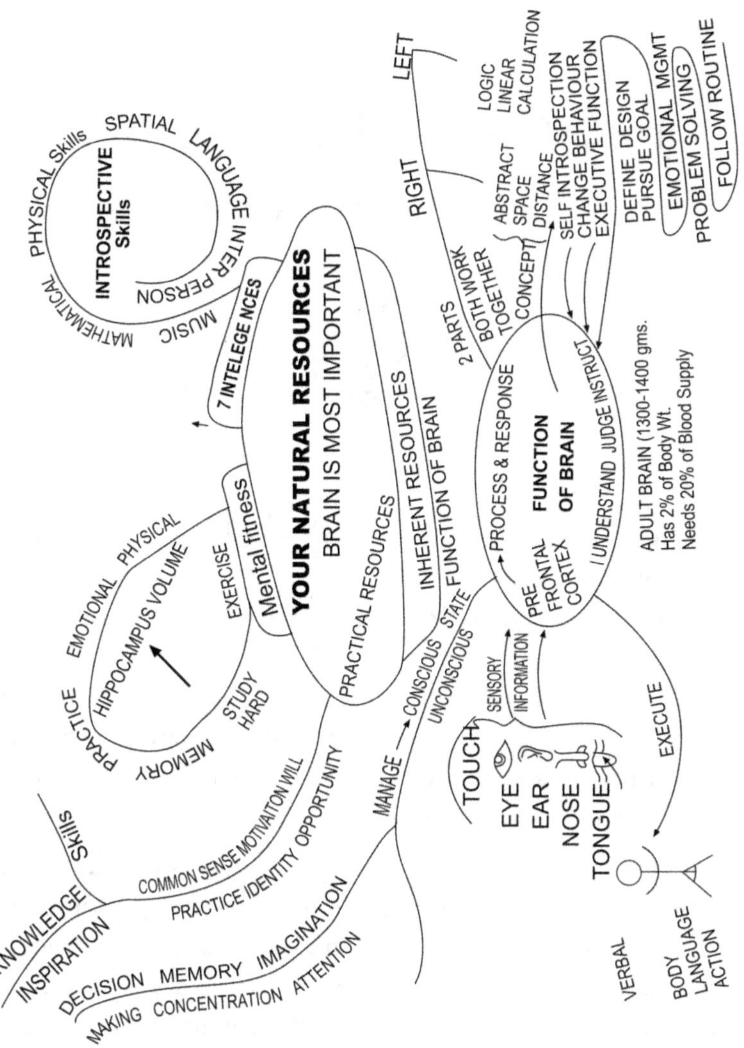

3

IRREVERSIBLE CHANGES IN ADOLESCENCE

Why and How

The period of adolescence extends from the age of 11 to 19 approximately. The changes occur in a scale not seen in any other phase of life. Like other animals, we undergo enormous physical, mental, emotional, sexual and psychological (behavioural) development. It makes us a mature adult. He or she is then able to fulfill the basic needs of life, namely, food, clothing, shelter, security, love, romance and reproduction.

It is the master, the pituitary gland in the skull which stimulates other hormonal glands to bring about this paradigm change. This results in extra secretion of growth, thyroid and adrenal hormones in both sexes. In male, sex hormone androgen and in the female, sex hormones estrogen and progesterone play their special role. They help in development of their respective sexual organs and shape psychological and emotional bend of mind.

Our genes control the time of release of all these hormones. Genes are also responsible for regulation of our longevity, skin colour, physique and proneness to specific diseases. We will consider these changes of adolescence in the above areas one by one.

Changes in BME

Changes occur in Body, Mind (which includes mentality, memory intelligence, psychology), Emotion and Sexuality. All these changes are meant to help you to become an adult individual.

Body: Physical changes are chiefly due to rapid release of thyroid and growth hormones in both the sexes—androgen hormones in males and estrogen and progesterone in females. Body structures enlarge in length and breadth. There is also an increase in all round strength and energy. There is an increase in the range and level of your activities. The height increases at the rate of 10 cm on an average per year in boys up to 18 years. In girls, it is at the rate of 9 cm per year up to 16 years. The growth depends on factors like genes, nutrition, etc. At first the head, hands and feet enlarge and then the adjoining parts of the limbs. Finally, the torso and shoulder shape your body (Adolescence http://en.wikipedia.org/wiki/adolescence, 12.2. 2014). Organs like brain, heart, liver, intestine, kidneys, lungs and their related systems also enlarge to gain the maturity and function of an adult. The Brain attains 90 per cent of adult size by the age of 6 years and full functional maturity is attained by 25 years. However, the brain can learn lifelong if you keep it active. The number of neurons in the brain is same in both the sexes. Males generally are taller, heavier and stronger than females.

Emotions: They are of two types—good and bad. Bad emotions are like hurting somebody's feelings by stealing or lying, being greedy, not doing one's duty, being lazy, arrogant, angry, violent or frightened. All these stimulate the body and mind to secrete harmful hormones like noradrenaline and cortisol. If such emotions are repeated over time, it can lead to illness. Good emotions, on the other hand, can make you happy and healthy. You experience it when you do something constructive. It can be to gain knowledge or any kind of skill or simply help others. Sharing and actually feeling others' joy and sorrow is empathy which is a good emotion. Visiting a place of natural beauty like riverside, ocean, mountain or jungle makes us happy. Helping somebody in distress, obeying elders, building self-esteem, helping others without accepting any favour in return, caring for family, society or your country makes you feel good as well. Wishing others well and ignoring short comings of others increase your store of good emotions. There is scientific proof that good thought or deeds keep you healthy through release of good hormones like Endorphins and Serotonin

Emotion is the most powerful member of BMETR. Have you heard of DasrathManjhi? If you haven't, then let me tell you his fantastic achievement. He chiseled off an area of 360 ft × 30 ft × 25 ft of a hill single-handedly with the help of only a chisel and hammer. His feat made way for a highway which benefitted the rural population of Sultanpur, Bihar. It brought schools, colleges, hospitals and more amenities many miles closer to the villagers. At first, people called him crazy but at the end Manjhi was revered as a messenger of God. This is an example not only of physical and mental strength but a triumph of service to humanity—the finest of all emotions!

Sexual: The changes are **Primary** or **Secondary** in Boys and Girls.

In girls, the primary sexual organs are a pair of ovary, a pair of fallopian tube, uterus and vagina, all of which are placed internally. They are present since birth. The beginning of adolescence in girls is marked by first menstruation called menarche. The ovaries gradually attain their adult size and function around 16 to 18 years of age. Secondary sexual changes in girls begin outwardly between 10 and 13 years of age approximately. It starts a year or two earlier than the boys and mostly ends a couple of years earlier. Girls have development of breasts, begin menstruation, have growth of hair in pubic and axillary areas, enlargement of hips and increase in height. They attain maximum heighttill18 yrs of age or so.

In boys, the primary sexual organ is a pair of testis which lies in each side of the scrotum. The testes gradually attain their adult size and function around 16 to 18 years of age. In boys, it is the first discharge of semen that marks the beginning of adolescence. Secondary sexual changes in boys include breaking of voice, increase in size of penis and scrotum, growth of pubic and axillary hair. Boys grow in height till 18 to 20 yrs.ofage.

The girls and boys both occasionally experience a wet dream. It is a normal, natural and a universal phenomenon. There is nothing to be ashamed or be perturbed about. This continues periodically. So, simply ignore it.

Attraction towards the opposite sex is a normal feature in adolescents as well as in adult. It takes a few more years to mature and understand and adjust to the familial and social norms of behaviour that is expected of us.

Mind: It functions as a nonstop working window of brain, expressing intelligence, desire, emotion and thoughts and ideas. Mind is restless and changes its narrative all the while. By keeping it in the present, it becomes relatively focused. The biggest advantage of mind is that it can see itself or the thoughts like a mirror. This is called introspection and is the key to develop intelligence and self-management. Feelings gradually mature and enable you to distinguish the nine emotions. They are joy, sorrow, anger, peace, valour, fear, surprise, romance and bizarre. By controlling, modifying or avoiding them you can improve your efficiency in whatever you do. It is good to keep disturbing emotions out while doing a job. You can also guess what others are feeling by observing their verbal and body language and respond accordingly. This ability to understand your own as well as others' feelings while interacting is emotional intelligence.

Mentality (psyche): is your opinion and attitude about the people, society, places and the world in general. It is formed by your interactions with inner and outer world over the years. You acquire a particular identity, sense of morality and self-esteem during this age. Psyche also includes concepts, opinion and beliefs about the idea of yourself, society and the world.

Executive function

Is a specialised form of application of Cognitive power. Cognition is the ability of the brain to recognise and process the information received through our special senses. It registers, processes and responds to them. It enables you to learn and respond to demands and challenges of life. Prefrontal cortex area of the brain is the seat of cognitive power.

It can be used to solve problems, or manage a situation in one's favour. Children at an age of 3–4 years gradually begin to acquire the ability to self-introspect, concentrate and carry out this important function. Examples of execeutive function for students are:

- To define, design and pursue a goal and stick to a routine to achieve it.
- Ability to shift your attention at will to what is more important.
- To be aware of any sensitive situation and coolly respond to it.
- Shut out the past and future and concentrate on the present work at hand.
- To be aware of your own and others' emotions while interacting and manage both, for your benefit.
- To remember names, maps, graphs, headings and the ability to comprehend and recall them at will.

- To be able to understand a new information or document and express it in your own words (comprehension)
- To face a stressful situation calmly and respond with maturity for the best outcome.
- To introspect and measure your progress from time to time in any field your BME is working on.

Psychosocial Issues

Attraction affects girls and boys due to hormonal changes in them. Psychologists say that romantic feelings between opposite sexes are natural and expected sequence of sexual maturity. Avoiding such distractions depends upon their inherent nature and ability to pursue their studies ignoring it. An environment of equality among the sexes is the modern concept of a healthy society. In co-educational institutions today, boys and girls interact and mingle normally. There should be fellow feeling, cooperation and respect as with friends of the same sex. Such modern institutional environment is going to be the norm in the coming years. This is due to awareness created by the society and educationists for wholesome development to adulthood. It will lead to recognition and acceptance of the opposite sex as equal and not sex objects. Such respect and attitude can eliminate the bias and disparity against a particular sex existing in schools, families and in professional or public life.

Acquaintances between boys and girls are meant to be kept within a decent and formal limit. It will keep their respective families free from anxiety. Crossing the limit can invite objection from them. This in turn may harm the personal, social, familial, financial interests of the students and their guardian's. In any case, in a few years of time, one will be more mature and self-reliant to be able to take a better decision on such matters.It is true that sexual urge can be disturbing at times. It may hinder a youth to pursue one's activities peacefully. From time immemorial, a vast majority of adolescents have been following their routine life in spite of it. Sexual urge finds an outlet through wet dreams in both sexes. It is a normal and harmless physiological process. One usually takes it in one's stride to ignore it. This is the best and healthiest solution. Some students are unable to withhold their sexual urge and resort to masturbation. There can be a sense of guilt of a compelling habit. To summarise, it is better to dedicate yourself completely to the pursuit of all the activities of student life and ignore the rest.

Friend circle: We tend to spend more time with friends as we grow up with them. We pick up the habits, mannerism and behaviour of our peers. There is an opportunity to build social contacts, a sense of belonging and security by making friends. One can develop a mature relationship with peers of both sexes as you grow up. It helps to make friends who are good at studies, with similar interests but without any bad habits. Such alliances can be maintained for many years and is mutually beneficial. The friendship can be lasting if one accepts them as they are.

Addiction: Adolescents, especially the males, are prone to pick up bad habits or become aggressive easily. This is due to hormonal (increase in androgen) changes. Hormones may also cause behavioural changes like risk taking and precipitate action. They usually affect your mind and intelligence and finally career and life. Its management is dealt elsewhere.

Swayed by a feeling of power with a group of friends, one may at times feel like a Bollywood hero and indulge in fights. Encouraged by success in smaller episodes, you may try bigger ones like ragging or bullying in schools. Some may acquire a tendency to commit worse crimes like extortion of money. Such behaviour, though uncommon, can lead one to even serious crimes. It may eventually attract the attention of the law and land you in a police station or a court. Bad company may be at the root of spoiling a promising career. So, it is better to choose well-behaved friends who are good at studies and have no addiction. It is better to accept power of adolescence gracefully, utilise for noble causes and avoid taking undue advantage.

Politics: Our country is governed under a democratic system. This allows people to raise their objection peacefully. Young men can object peacefully to any existing condition if they disagree. Their receptive and idealistic mind revolts easily against rampant social evils, corruption and injustice. To correct the situation, a legal system is in place which isnot able to cope with the number of cases registered in a reasonable time frame. This is due to shortage of number of judicial officers and judges.In some colleges, the adult students have unions. They often create unrest. This affects the academic atmosphere adversely in general and those actively involved in it in particular.

There is no harm to know about the policies of political parties and their leaders. But for a student who wants to pursue his studies and career seriously, it is wise to stay away from political activities or violence. It may affect your study and performance in examinations which is your task at hand. The truth is that education and knowledge counts in one's career even if it is going to be politics in the long run.

Legal issues: It is something we should be aware of. You become a major after completing 18 years of age, thereby, becoming an adult in the eyes of law. Prior to attaining majority, you are governed by juvenile law and juvenile court. Between the age of 7 and 18, different levels of charges may be filed depending on the type of crime the juveniles commit. If found guilty, the juvenile may be kept in a remand home and given a chance to reform himself/herself. It is, therefore, much safer to keep away from any wrong doing because more than the legal punishment it will be a serious blot on one's character, self-esteem and disrupt your studies. It will even remain as a painful memory.

Law allows some privileges to an adult. You are eligible to vote only after completing 18 years of age. This landmark age of 18 years also allows you to accept employment or get admitted in a professional college. You can also sign contracts or accept employment. Law requires you to complete 21 years (age varies from 18 to 21 in some states) before you can consume alcoholic drink or drive a car. Any violation of above rules may invite legal action and may spoil your character certificate and career. The age of 18 makes the girls are eligible to marry of their own choice. For boys, the eligibility to marry is 21 or 22 in India. Majority of modern youth, however, are practical. They prefer not to marry till they can support a family.

Negative Tendencies

Risk Taking: The adolescent decade is notorious for this. Youths perform stunts, take selfies (photo with mobile camera) in dangerous spots or hang precariously in running local trains. They indulge in speeding the cars or two wheelers beyond permissible limits. 60 per cent of accidents occur due to ignoring the prescribed speed limits. They violate traffic rules and do not wear helmets while on a motor cycle or get involved in brawls and road rage. As may be expected, they get injured frequently and often critically. Besides, they injure others as well. They can be taken to the police station, hospital or even jail. Their family has to bear the misery and cost of this indiscretion. At present, more than a lakh of commuters die due to road traffic accidents every year. Majority of them are young. Many of the accidents are due to a sudden gush of Androgen, a male hormone, which creates aggressive behaviour.

I was 14 years old when I used to sneak out of my home at 5 AM when all family members were asleep. They were unaware of my escapade. I used to join my friends and walk a couple of kilometers to learn swimming in the River Gandak in Bihar. I used to return in an hour by scaling the wall and then go back to bed. In due course, I could swim independently. However, there was a shock in store for us swimmers. One expert swimmer, who was our coach cum friend, had drowned—by getting caught in a whirlpool. The tragic news devastated us. For a long time, we blamed ourselves and felt guilty about our escapades.

Mood Swing: It is another negative effect of psychological turmoil. Sometimes, sensitive children feel happy and sometimes sad without a good enough reason. It may come following praise or a scolding from guardian or teacher. The aggrieved can get over such miseries by talking to friends or family about the problem for a solution. One can get busy with some other activity of interest to forget and heal the hurtful moments. These are in any case transitory. Physical exercise and yoga are really helpful in such situations to get back their equanimity. A few fail to overcome the psychological hurt and suffer. Severe Depression occurs in a sensitive mind. It hits them hard, leading to a state of hopelessness. The sufferer can even consider the extreme step of suicide on the spur of the moment. This possibility should be kept in mind by guardians, teachers, friends and others. Their compassionate interaction with the young ones can go a long way to assuage their feelings of hurt and prevent such calamities. Many failures of the youngsters are temporary and can be corrected. However, it can be the syndrome called 'Depression' which needs proper treatment. Teachers and guardians should, therefore, be careful in dealing with students in general and avoid severe scolding or punishment to known sensitive individuals.

Positive Thinking

Disappointment and sufferings are inevitable part of everybody's life. What matters is how you respond to it. Most can face it as a challenge to be resolved by positive thinking and action. This can convert an apparent distress or failure into a flying success. All have an inherent ability to overcome an unfavourable situation by pondering on it and find a solution. Any setback is, after all, temporary. We have to be alert to prevent any adverse situation. We can commit not to do the same mistake twice. One can seek advice from a friend, well wisher or a teacher in case of doubt.

My experience: Diphtheria, a critical throat infection, was prevalent in late 1960s. It has now been brought under control by immunisation. One winter night, I was asleep in my quarter, adjacent to the hospital. The sound of many footsteps in the staircase woke me up. I heard a rhythmic whistling sound and it dawned on me that it could be Diphtheria. This infection in throat can choke the wind pipe, leading to this typical sound. Such cases used to come for emergency surgical intervention. I rushed out of my room and saw a six-month old infant having acute difficulty in breathing. Her lips had turned blue.

I explained to the parents that her critical condition needed urgent surgery. They agreed, and we rushed to the hospital operation theatre (O.T). I made a hole in the wind-pipe and fixed a metal tube within. Instantly, the baby started breathing normally, allowing me to go back to my slumber.

After a few weeks, the baby was called inside the O.T. for removal of the metal tube which I removed. However, I noticed that all was not well. She was in acute breathing distress again. She stopped breathing gradually and her body turned blue. I tried to revive (by inserting the tube) but failed. I went out and declared the patient dead. Then, all of a sudden, I felt an urge to try to put the tube back again as a last resort. This time I was successful and continued resuscitation procedures. Luckily the baby started breathing normally to my surprise and joy.

Later, I thought about what might have prevented the tube to enter the wind pipe on my first attempt. One of the explanations could be that later her throat muscles had relaxed in a near-death situation. This made it easier for me to insert the pipe. Now the worrying question was when to remove the tube again without any risk?

I consulted my mentor on phone and followed his advice by preparing the patient with some medication. After a few weeks, the tube removal was eventless. I was delighted. But I was overwhelmed with joy when after 16 years, the teenager came just to thank me. The whole episode taught me two things—one, never say no to legitimate challenges and two, seek help from seniors. In difficult situation, just say, 'Yes, I can and I will.' This mental posture is the way to overcome obstacles.

Think of the attitude of the girl Sudha Chandran, who lost one of her legs but continued giving dance recitals on Indian stage. Imagine, Chandrashekar, with a deformed bowling hand, was the ace spinner of Indian cricket team. The world's foremost astrophysicist, Stephen Hawking, spent greater part of his life tied to a wheel-chair. Yet he continued with path-breaking research work until his death recently. There are myriad others who have faced life's setbacks but responded differently with success.

Ingenuity of an Adolescent

On 2 October 2015, I was watching a video recording of a South African jungle scene on the Discovery channel. A lion's family(called 'PRIDE') was resting with a huge male lion and two watchful lionesses pacing leisurely nearby. Lionesses, as you might know, are better hunters than the lions and are respected by the family members. There were two restless cubs (twins) who were teasing and playing with their parents.

An official video team often visits the same animal groups periodically to study their habitat, health and behaviour. When the members revisited the family after a lapse of time, they were surprised and even worried by the absence of the two cute lively cubs. But somebody suggested that the big cats invariably force their adolescent offsprings out of their domain. The young cubs then are forced to fend for their own safety and seek food water and shelter elsewhere. This challenging law of jungle creates a training period for the young ones to become a self-reliant adult. The video team accepted this possibility and searched the nearby and distant jungles for the missing duo. They specially searched places where there was a water outlet because all living beings are dependent on it.

They soon found the now grown up cubs who seemed to have lost weight and their sheen. It was apparent that they were hungry and had lost their comfort zone. They were slowly moving towards a small lake for water to drink when two elephants charged them. The hapless twins sprinted to safety. Next day appeared to be more favourable as they chanced upon a dead rhinoceros cub near a bush. Hardly had they started their breakfast, that one parent rhino rushed towards them. They had to run for their lives again. Even though by now they were young lions, they could not match the big animals. They also lacked the hunting skills of an adult. It was their bad luck that they had not come across smaller animals so far to kill and hone their hunting skill.

Later, having regained some energy, they returned to reclaim their food. This time the vigilant adult rhino again rushed towards one of them. The chase took both of them far and away. The other lion had cleverly hidden himself behind a tree as they had planned. He was quick to drag the dead rhino cub to an opposite direction. This intelligent planning of getting the dead rhino far from the old site had worked well for them. On return of the first lion, both of them had a hearty meal in peace. They had learnt a new hunting strategy—'necessity is the mother of invention'.

Mind Map 3: IRREVERSIBLE CHANGES OBSERVED IN ADOLESCENCE

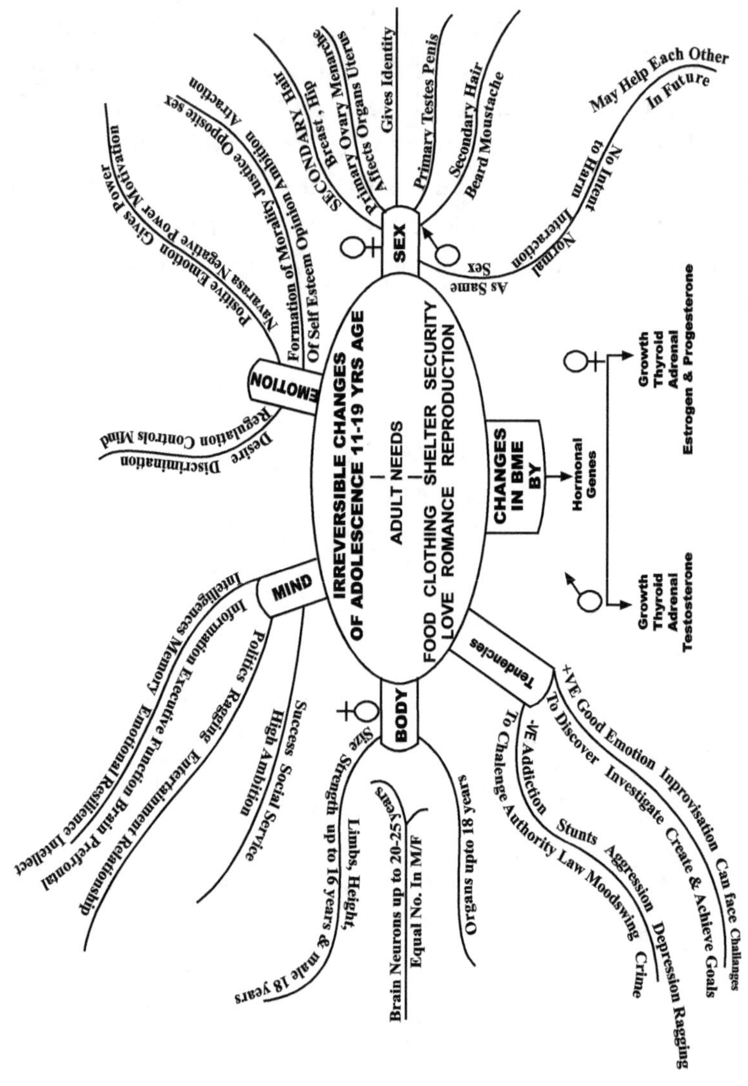

4

MANTRA OF BMETR

Understanding BMETR and Mantra

BMETR: Our body, mind, emotion, time and routine make a tidy group of five which influences our personality and life. I have named it BMETR for convenience. The first letter of the five words have been joined in that order to coin this acronym. Now let us consider what mantra means with respect to BMETR.

Mantra: Paramahansa Yogananda in his world-famous *Autobiography of a Yogi* (1945, Page 462) has termed mantra as 'Instrument of thought.' Mantra is a repetitive statement of humble and sincere request to a higher power to grant one's desired objective. It is practised daily at a given time and place when alone. Mantras are believed to be effective if one follows his karma honestly, without harming anybody. Mantra literally means that which gives relief (तराण) to mind (मन)from fear and sorrow.

In the BMETR context, the request to the higher power is made in the form of use, action or exercise. This will improve the quality, strength and energy of BMETR to a desired level. Mantra is thus more than a verbal request. It is a prayer, sincere desire, leading to an effort in the form of exercise—all rolled into one. Adolescence is the appropriate time to giveone's life a proper direction.

In the chapter of Routine, an hour in the early morning has been specially allotted for exercise of this mantra. This one hour each day may prove to be the axle of your life cart. In the following hours of the day too, you will be exercising the BMETR Mantra in different ways, such as, by studying which is exercising the intellect and so on.

Now we will try to understand BMETR in details, one by one:

The first member of BMETR, BODY is one that you can see or touch but the other four you cannot. The body happens to be the abode of the rest four and carries out instructions.

MIND is the second member through which our consciousness, desire, discrimination and intellect, with the help of memory, operate.

EMOTION is the third and most powerful member. It examines the information we receive and helps us in decision making and action.

TIME happens to be the fourth of the lot. It is unique because it can be perceived only through the sun or through a timekeeper like watch. This is the only member which you cannot control. So, you are compelled to adjust all your activities according to it.

ROUTINE is the last one. It is the time package of 24 hours at your disposal to be spent as you wish. Spending it wisely is the key to succeed in life.

All five members are intimately related to each other. If you have a single member indisposed, the rest are affected. As for example, during fever, all the rest of the members will be unwilling to comply or cooperate. Unhealthy food if taken for a long time proves to be unhealthy for all the members sooner or later.

It is only through an efficient BMETR that you can achieve your goals. All normal human beings have equal potential to succeed in life.

We will discuss how to keep BMETR in the best of health and spirit one by one.

Body and Wellness

This three-dimensional structure is your unique identity among the seven billion plus population of the world. It is in our own interest that we keep the body in a healthy condition. Good health is not only absence of diseases but also presence of adequate strength, energy, ability to work and enjoy a long, meaningful life. Body is an asset which can enable you to study harder to get better marks. If good in sports and games, one will get preference in admission. If gifted in it, he can aspire to represent in national or international levels. Sports and games are enriching pastime. A daily 'looking after' of the body, exercise and no addiction keeps it in good condition. Even a robot requires periodic check up and maintenance.

Genes and immunity are important factors for good health. Good health also depends on clean surroundings, healthy food and drink, no addictions, regular habits, minimal mental stress, healthy lifestyle and daily exercise. Cleanliness and prompt medical advice can keep diseases away. By immunization, many infective diseases can be prevented right from infancy. Timely intervention can cure diseases. All these measures increase resistance against diseases. Later, even their future generations are very likely to inherit their good genes. Just imagine how attractive a healthy youth looks, standing straight. One can almost feel the positive energy in him or her.

Environment: A pollution-free environment is a necessity for good health. It prevents many diseases. Sadly, this is not so in most of our towns and cities at present. The Environment is responsibility of the state. At present it is in need of public education and active participation by all. It will be a good idea if you, with some friends, decide to improve cleanliness and hygienic condition of the area you live in. Living rooms need ventilation (windows) and sunlight. Hygienic toilets with water supply, adequate drainage and purification system are important to protect one. One can form a group and work on waste disposal, cleanliness, emission of smoke in one's neighborhood areas and discourage addiction at home or in society. Polluted air is responsible for many diseases like asthma, cancer and heart diseases. Impure water causes infective, abdominal and nervous system diseases, e.g., diarrhoea, enteric fever and Japanese encephalitis. All these diseases are preventable. One should guard against extremes of temperature to avoid ill health. It is well known that planting trees and ensuring their maturity is a social and praiseworthy service. It helps environment, gives shelter to birds, controls temperature and produces oxygen. It contributes to our good health, provides fruits and products of medicinal value.

Food and drink: Your health largely depends on what you eat or drink. A balanced diet, physical and mental exercise prevents many diseases like diabetes, high blood pressure, heart disease, obesity, dementia and helps us to live long. These ailments are increasing alarmingl y in our country. A balanced diet comprises of adequate calories and carbohydrate, protein, fat, vitamins, minerals like zinc, calcium and manganese. Please develop taste for green vegetables and fruits, specially the seasonal ones. Restrict oil or fat, salt, sugar and spices. Avoid fast foods and aerated drinks. It is better not to consume food or drinks exposed to unhygienic condition. Avoid taking food or drink kept exposed to open air, dirt and insects. Tinned food or bottled sweet drinks or fruit juices are harmful because of the added preservatives and artificial colour. It is better to eat 4–5 times a day including a heavy breakfast. See that you don't get an overloaded stomach. This will not let you concentrate on study as the blood is diverted to digestive organs. It is also better to avoid strenuous activity like exercise and games within 2 hours of a full meal. Following the above guideline will promote good health. One has to restrict calorie intake if one has a tendency to become overweight.

Please take care to drink filtered, boiled or potable pure water. A total daily intake of water should be usually 2 to 3 litre even in winter. In summer or after strenuous activity, one may need more. This ensures a normal urinary output of around 1500 ml of urine per 24 hrs. Please take care not to use dirty water for drinking or even for washing clothes or utensils.

The bulk of the two main, standard meals at lunch and dinner include roti/ rice, pulses or saambhar and plenty of green vegetables. At the end, milk or yoghurt with jaggery (gur) will give good energy and digestion. Pulses (daal), egg, meat (chicken or fish), soybean, paneer (cottage cheese), rajma and beans are good sources of protein and one of these should be taken daily. A meal served in a middle class Indian household is usually a healthy one.

Plenty of seasonal fruits and vegetables are desirable. Seasonal fruits like banana, mango, jackfruit, guava, apples, pears, plums, melons, etc. are very nutritious. Salads comprising raw tomato, onions, radish, carrots and other veggies are full of antioxidants. These are helpful to keep the brain and heart healthy and also give you vitality.

To summarise, restrict intake of oil and fat, red meat, animal fat, salt and sugar. Avoid preserved or packaged food and drinks. Beware of exposed food kept in dirty and congested market places. Animal organs like liver, kidney, brain and fast food, noodles and pizza are also harmful. Fish is healthier and it has good fat. Evidence in animals and humans prove that repeated consumption of high fat and sugar diets lead to specific impairments of the hippocampus which underpin the consequent changes in cognition—SobeskyJL (2014) et. al.

❖ Diet during intensive study: A heavy meal makes one drowsy and hampers study and concentration. A schedule of eating light, 5 to 6 times from 7 AM to 9 PM in moderate quantities is helpful. Reducing cereals and adding more fruit, vegetables and yoghurt will help you study more. It is better to follow a routine and morning exercise for an hour is helpful for intense study. A growing adolescent needs as much calories as an adult.

❖ Lifestyle: There is consensus that a good lifestyle has multiple benefits. It helps to reduce stress. Food, drink and sleep in proper time has been a time honoured practice. A regular life makes it a balanced, dynamic and successful one. Getting up early, say at five in the morning, and going to bed at nine has been recommended by lifestyle coaches. A timely heavy breakfast and two lighter meals with snacks in between have been recommended. Seven to eight hours of sleep is adequate to let the brain and body rest to recover fully.

❖ Prevention of Accidents: It is better to avoid congested places or busy roads if you can. Observe traffic rules of high-speed limits, zebra crossing and helmets. By observing traffic rules, you can avoid road accidents which kills more than a hundred thousand travelers per year, specially the younger ones.

❖ Energy: Generally, children and adolescents are full of it because they are eager to experience new things and are free from worldly responsibility. Keep a watch on your well being. Feeling unwell for a few days could be due to some anxiety or health issues.

Such feelings do occur in life. They test your patience and intelligence. You can investigate your BMETR for a clue like an expert detective. However, please do not hesitate to seek medical help if necessary.

❖ Longevity: The average longevity of Indians is now around 68 years and is likely to go up. Long and healthy life gives you the opportunity to achieve more.

❖ Addiction: I have seen many families ruined by addiction to alcohol. smoking, chewing tobacco, paan (Betel leaf, nuts, etc.). One can prevent this by a solemn promise of not touching any addictive substances ever. This can be the single best decision of your life.

In a nutshell:

- Ensure adequate nutrition.
- Say no to addiction.
- Have 7–8 hours of sleep.
- Exercise regularly.
- Keep an eye on your height and weight ratio.

Physical Exercise

Working out the body, mind and emotions have been in practice for thousands of years in our country. However, scientific proof has been forthcoming in the last few decades only.

Exercise can be done for the body as a whole or with special emphasis to any limb, organ or body parts. It is done repeatedly to make them stronger. A continued body effort which increases your respiratory and heart rate will make both of them healthy. The internet site http://w.w.w.preventdiseases.com (2012) says—regular physical exercise in children yields similar benefits as in adults. This has received wide acclaim, as it helps youngsters develop their body, mind and emotions.

In 1949, Jerry Morris and his team were the first to prove that since bus drivers do not move much, they are more prone to heart attacks. The bus conductors suffer from this disease much less frequently. This is because conductors are on their feet and move constantly. This has been mentioned in a Wikipedia 2012 article and in Lancet (1953) by Morris J.N. et al. in an article 'Coronary Heart Disease and Physical Activity or Work.' http://en.wikipedia.org/wiki/physicalexercise.

The Benefits of Exercise:

It helps in gaining physical strength, skill, stamina, bone strength, body flexibility, balance, movement with accuracy, speed and coordination, energy, good health (prevents diabetes, heart diseases) and ensures longer lifespan. They have a feeling of wellness due to hormone Endorphin.

Types of Physical Exercise:

1. Aerobic: in which the oxygen supply is adequate for example brisk walking and cycling. The effort improves the strength of muscle. You are able to talk while doing it. It can be difficult if you increase the speed of exercise. It is more popular and is good for your heart and lungs. Yoga like asana, pranayama and dhyana are also helpful. However, unlike aerobic exercise they slow down the heart and respiration rate. A combination of both is desirable. It can preferably be done for one hour each day on an average but can be adjusted to eighty-four minutes five days a week compensating for the lost time.

2. *Anaerobic:* It is more strenuous than aerobic exercise. In this form there is temporary deficiency of oxygen supply to meet the demand of body. The examples are weight training or running fast for a long duration. It has much quicker and more visible effect on the muscle mass, heart and lungs. You cannot talk during this effort. It is not suitable for older people. Weaklings become stronger with supervised graded anaerobic exercise.

3. *Stretching:* Resistant exercise, stretching and asana are a variant of aerobic effort. It helps muscles by elongating them by some counteracting force. It helps flexibility of muscle and joint. There is a saying that you are as young as you are flexible. (Brinkin, 1995. http://www.preventdisease.com/fitness/fitkids/ARTICLES/benefit-fitness-on-childrenhtml) has established that regular exercise is also good for stimulating brain. There is increase in overall strength, academic performance and attitude towards school. It improves blood supply and nutrients to the whole body including the brain.

Summary of Benefits of Exercise:

- Prevention of diseases of the lungs, blood vessels and heart and brain
- Decreases bad hormones like cortisol and nor adrenaline.

- Increases good hormones like Endorphin and serotonin
- Regulates sleep, body weight, mental health and depression.
- Improves body's immune system.
- Increases energy, enthusiasm and cheerfulness.
- Physical exercise increases memory and brain function.
- It gives our body an attractive and healthy look.

It Improves strength, longevity and self confidence. It has been demonstrated thatvigorous aerobic exercise has multiple benefits in school going children William B Strong et.al.(2005) It prevents diseases and cardiovascular, cognitive and superior motor (Musculo- skeletal) fitness in children who regularly exercise. They also are better in studies and have positive attitude towards schools. Ross and Pate in 1987 showed that physically fit children have fewer cardiovascular risk factors than less active children (http://w.w.w.preventdiseases,com) Please note that physical fitness also boosts mental and emotional health.

Since my childhood, I was fond of sports and games. This continued till my medical college days. Later, when I was posted at Begusarai (Bihar), a district town in 1974 I longed for some physical activity. So, I resorted to cycling for going to work to the government hospital and my private clinic. The public was unaccustomed to see a doctor on a cycle in those days and used to comment. However, I continued to cycle till I was seventy-one. Some other doctors also started cycling to work. Now it is well known that physical activity also contributes towards mental fitness. Later, I continued exercising and I am fit in my early eighties.

Mind and Mentality

The mind is the channel for conscious flow of thoughts, intellect, emotions, discrimination, desire and imagination. We will discuss them and their exercises.

Mind: requires to be strengthened by physical exercise and specific exercises of a different kind, such as meditation, yoga, trataka and reciting numbers after adding on in ascending or descending order which upgrade attention, concentration, cognition and memory (see next page of this chapter for details).

Mind is like a television screen. It has three available channels. The three are—present, past and future. A full attention to the *present* channel is the most desirable one. An awareness of *now* and its related thought, speech or activity or task at hand is productive. If you can stick to this form of mental exercise then you may reach great heights. The *future* channel is good for planning. But limit yourself to only the major things you need to achieve. The future can be thought of to plan for an important event or goal to achieve. The *past* channel is helpful only if it reminds you of lessons learnt. Please remember the lesson but forget the rest because it is dead and worthless. All this sounds simple but is actually difficult to follow. As in dhyana, whenever the mind uses the past or future channels, switch them off and bring your mind or attention back to the present again. This needs to be repeated till the attention is focused on a single object. This is the mental exercise to eliminate distraction which will make your faculty of attention strong.

Intellect: is an overall brain function assisted by attention, cognition, memory and knowledge. All these help the prefrontal cortex to reach a decision for action. There is an excellent book on this subject titled *The Sharp Brains Guide to Brain Fitness* by Alvaro Fernandez and ElkhononGoldber and Pascale Michelon (2013).

The seven intelligences (See Chapter 2) can be used selectively with preference for the ones which are important for preparation of examination.

Essentials of a good intellect:

- To have a good knowledge of your mother tongue and a second language.
- A legible and neat handwriting is a must.
- To comprehend written material and then express it in your own words is a good practice. An ability to translate it into another language is a desirable skill.
- To learn a 3rd language will take you to a higher level of intelligence.
- Arithmetic or Mathematics add to your clarity, concentration and problem-solving capacity.
- Self introspection helps emotional management and to concentrate in study by minimizing internal distraction.
- The book *Sharp Brains* (2013), page 166 in a research involving 1000 people, quotes that

meditation reduces anxiety, and has a profound effect on attention and cognition in both children and adults.

- The famous neuroscientist, Ryuita Kawashima, in his book *Train Your Brain* (2016) states that one digit of simple addition, subtraction or division can improve your attention in a few seconds. He has recommended it before study.

- Even if your main interest is in other subjects, keep in touch with Arithmetic and its tables.

- The intelligence can be honed by being alert to the inputs of your senses and by keeping your attention glued to the present moment.

- Concentration can be increased by continuously gazing at a point on the wall daily for about 10 minutes. It is called 'Trataka'. Pranayama and Dhyana are also effective tools.

- Problem-solving skill is aided by Sudoku, different kind of puzzles, spelling quizzes, crossword, chess and detective stories.

- You can apply your mind to solve problems in study and other things. In a game like football, one can plan by assessing the player's competence and suitability in a particular position. Their running or tackling ability, stamina, defense, passing skills are worth considering. You can even plan a pre-game strategy for scoring a goal. You can overcome hurdles in daily life or study by applying similar principles. This is a way to improve quality of life.

- The brain is the most important organ. Brain fitness depends on physical exercise, adequate sleep, doing new things, solving problems, healthy food, absence of intoxicants and stress. Frequent challenges to the brain to solve problems increase neuroplasticity.

- Social engagement, emotional resilience and cognitive engagement like learning, make the brain fit.

- Challenging your intellect: Please refer to the book *Mental Fitness* by Tom Wujec (2011) for more of such mental exercise, 2x2 is 4. Then multiply 4 with 2, you get 8, go on multiplyig with 2 without a stop and see how far you can go. Try to go further to improve your capability to multiply. Take 1 and 2 as unit and go on adding 2 and 3 respectively to each digit without a stop till you reach 200. Then descend by subtracting 2 and 3 respectively till you reach 1 and 2 again.

Play with numbers. If you take 6 and 7 as unit, add 3 to each and you get 9 and 10. Go on adding up 1 to 3 to each respectively, it becomes 10 and 12. Keep playing till you get 200. Then subtract similarly, till you come back to where you started, i.e., 6 and 7. It will improve your short-term memory.

- If you are a right-handed person, practise to use your left hand instead of right, e.g., writing, dressing up, washing your clothes, etc.

- Make a rhyme of a small lesson to remember it easily.

- Make a sketch of your home and neighbourhood and of the road leading to your school.
- Draw the plan of the house you are living in. All this will upgrade your spatial memory.

Discrimination: We use this faculty every day. We become a better person by sticking to norms of good behavior. You choose the good option and discard the bad, by applying your discrimination. Examples are, to speak the truth, not to hurt any living being, to obey the elders, not to steal or use unfair means in examination or in any walk of life, not to fight, etc. All this keeps you safe from any danger or crime. It helps to avoid distractions or bad company or enemies who can harm you. It helps in academic performance.

Emotion

There are good emotions like selfless service, doing good to others and helping anybody in distress. There are bad emotions which can hurt not only others but also oneself. There is an example of John Hunter, a pioneer of modern medicine and surgery, who fell dead when he exploded in anger for the bad workmanship of a carpenter. Biochemical changes show that the good ones release good hormones like endorphins and serotonin which make you cheerful and healthy. The bad emotions like violence, envy and fear cause a flow of damaging hormones. They may cause diseases and acute condition like a heart attack in the long run I too had a bad experience, remaining in a state of anxiety for months till the matter was resolved.

Once a young man was operated for appendix and was admitted in my clinic. As was the norm, the doctor on night duty went to see him. The patient was doing well but due to some misunderstanding between the patient's father and doctor, there was an altercation. The father abused and threatened the doctor.

Next morning when I went to clinic, I was informed about the episode. I promptly called the father of the patient, who was an advocate. I was angry because of his behaviour and asked for an explanation. The father was aggressive and threatened me too. I lost my cool. The neighbours present there supported me and rebuked the advocate. The matter ended for the time being.

After a while, I heard that the advocate had left the clinic with the patient in a huff, without informing anyone. Later I came to know that he had lodged a case against me for criminal negligence. He had alleged that the condition of his patient was deteriorating, and he was not being attended by the doctor. As a result, he was compelled to take the patient to another doctor. This doctor's prescription mentioned admission and intravenous fluid and other measures he had taken. Later, it was known that the doctor had given a false statement. But I was put in a unfavourable situation. My well-wishers and other senior doctors approached the advocate and pressurised him to withdraw the case. Finally, the case was withdrawn, but not before someone else had to apologise on my behalf in my presence. However, this episode was an insult and punishment for me. It taught me that one should not lose temper in a stressful situation. One should consult friends and other professionals first before reacting.

Anger is your worst enemy. It releases bad hormones, namely, adrenaline, noradrenalin and cortisol. These affect the brain and the rest of the body adversely. In a fit of rage all of a sudden you feel as if you possess superhuman power. You feel stronger but lose orientation, clarity and common sense. You follow the primitive reflex response of fight or flight, thus, leaving the actual problem unattended.

You can manage a grave situation or anger resulting from your or somebody else's fault by adopting Traffic light formula on the spot.

Red: Stand quietly. Be alert, still and conscious of the place, time and people. Count your breath till you are composed. Keep your attention on your breath indefinitely. If anybody could help, then ring him.

Yellow: Calmly and without any bias try to figure out the cause of the situation and its consequences. If the situation allows then try to negotiate with the help of others. If you are at fault, then admit it and apologize.

Green: If the matter is settled in your favour, leave immediately. If things are getting worse for you, then run away immediately.

Anger or Stressful experience in any form overtime can cause diabetes, high blood pressure, heart ailments, loss of memory, cancer and other diseases. It harms you and others' BMETR. It can spoil your day, career or even your life.

Emotional Management

I may point out to all my young friends that these nine years feel like a bullet train journey from the adolescent junction to adulthood terminus. So safe guard your main interest, which is your career, first. In the free time, enjoy the unique wayside passing scenery and company of fellow passengers. The experience will enrich you but beware of the wayside hazards and occasional unsavory fellow travelers. Use your tact, wit, common sense and maturity to deal with co-passengers while you enjoy the journey.

One way to control bad emotion is to behave with others as you would expect others to behave with you. One can eliminate a lot of tension when you speak the truth and ignore fault of others. Emotional exercise has been mentioned in the chapter on Routine.

We should occasionally visit parks, rivers, sea beach or a place of scenic beauty to enjoy nature. These places uplift you. It gives you peace and joy which lasts longer than worldly pleasures. One can enjoy television or films which are thought-provoking, instructive and entertaining once a fortnight or so.

Time Management

Our body is physiologically adjusted by our Hypothalamus of brain according to sun. It is called circadian rhythm and the effect on us is called body clock. Nature has gifted us a treasure of time but it will vanish with our last breath. So the wise, plan and manage this invisible, invaluable, unstoppable, non-negotiable capital to be spent totally but thoughtfully. I have suggested a sample of routine about how a single day can be spent to our advantage. One's success in life largely depends on how well you manage a day, every day.

One can make a to-do list daily about the study task and other jobs according to priority. Sometimes important task is missed if you do not write it down and look it up in the morning and at bedtime.

Yearly Time Table

Preparation for yearly examination should proceed in a regular and calculated manner which should preferably end a month before its date of commencement. This allows time for repeated review and strengthening of the weak areas.

Let us discuss briefly how to appraise the yearly task load of all subjects. This has to be assessed in the perspective of time available in a yearly and weekly frame. Though it appears to be daunting at first but with the help of teachers you can do it. In case the syllabus is well defined it will be easy. If vague or undefined then one has to assess the text books, question papers, MCQs or ask teacher's advice and do it. It will help to assess your task ahead in each subject. You can then estimate your preparedness any time.

First measure the task, i.e., the syllabus to be covered in 11 months in a year. Then calculate the time we have for study each day. Assess the subjects in syllabus as the total task against the days and study hours including regular and the extra hours available on holidays. Keep a margin for days lost when you won't be able to study due to illness or other engagements. One important principle is to divide a big task into small manageable chunks and divide them into two or three categories. The three categories of the study task are, very important, important and not-so-important. We should know everything about the first category, 50 percent of the second and only a concept and outline of the unimportant ones. Keep last one month before yearly examination for extensive revision.

Time available: One must find out how much time one requires to prepare a standard piece of task in each subject. You can then apportion time for them accordingly. All this may appear complicated but such an assessment will give you an idea of the task per week and confidence to cover the syllabus and study.

Then, prepare a *weekly* time table for study every week, subject-wise, from the monthly share of the total task of the year. This will help you to monitor the rate of progress closely. Ensure that the whole syllabus is covered four weeks prior to the start of examination. This will give time to take care of the un-prepared lessons and review the entire syllabus. Review is an important part of study and extensive review shortly before examination is crucial.

The weekly time table includes subjects, allotment of their time including the review. It has to be followed regularly from day one of the beginning of session. A realistic approach is important. Please assess the time you will take to study first time by SQ3R Method and prepare its review material. One should follow the schedule for a month to know the merit of weekly plans. Assess your preparedness every month end. This will tell where you stand in the path of preparation.

Mind Map 4: MANTRA OF BMETR

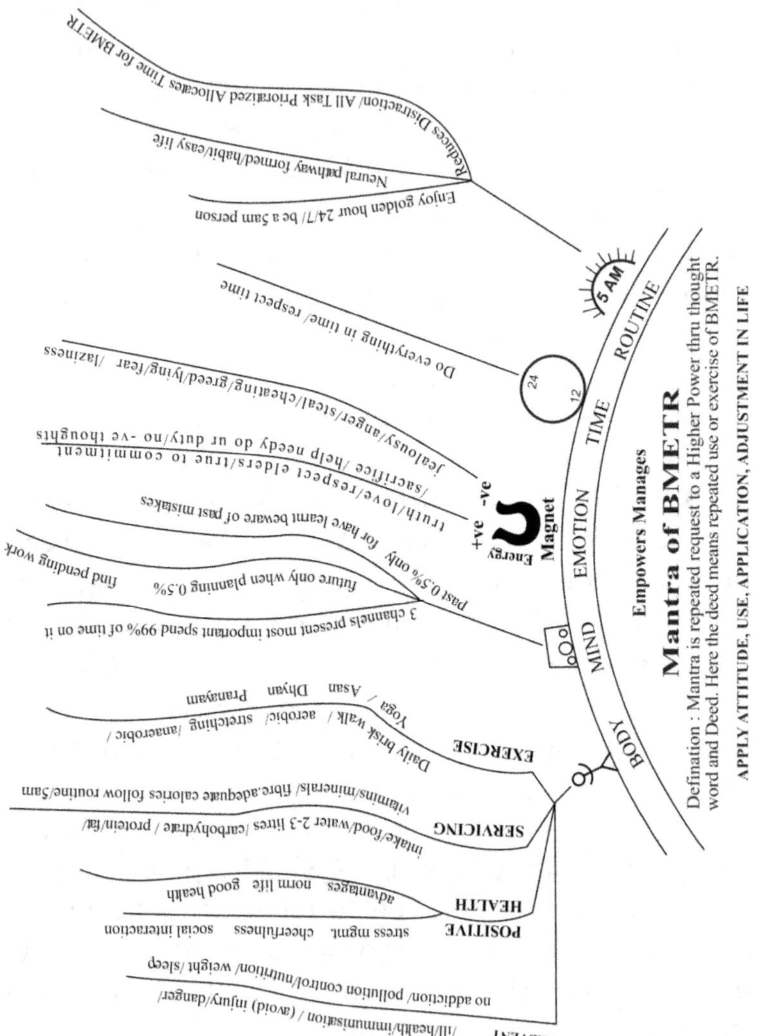

<u>5</u>

AMBITION AND DREAMS

Why Fixing a GoalIs a Vital Decision?

- **Deeply motivates to achieve the goal**
- **Defines a road map for it**
- **To meet the basic requirements of life.**
- **Disciplines BMETR**
- **Gives meaning to life**

To choose the appropriate career of your liking at school is a landmark decision. However, a correct decision can be made with a planned approach and some research. First, ask yourself which five subjects or professions you like the most and write them in order of preference. It will, first of all, require choosing appropriate subjects compatible with the intended careers. Then work out the compatibility between subjects and professions. Revise the list after cancelling the incompatible ones. The list will be shorter now. Find out which of the professions are close to your heart because this is the most important factor. You are young and may not be well informed about careers and professions. Keep a tentative list in waiting. Then, initiate discussion with parents, teachers, well-wishers and senior friends about it. You can get a feasible and practical idea from concerned professionals as well. Consult books and the net about the options available. Get some idea about existing employment, career and profession's scenario. You may keep two or three options open and cancel the rest. This decision will bring relief and stimulate you to study with vigour. You will look forward to the admission test of related professional college later. By the time you are in the senior class, your results will finally tell you what to choose. There are some students who are clear about their choice right from the start and are smart enough to search and decide their career. They donot need other's help. They deserve special applause for being so clear and decisive at such a young age.

You may look up in the net about newer avenues like branches of electronics, cyber security, block chain (computer science), artificial intelligence (A.I or Machine intelligence), robotics, machine learning (An upcoming branch dealing with machine operation), space engineering, environmental science, Nanoscience and technology and animation. Look for overseas colleges and scholarships or study loans. Such brainstorming will help to know your mind and opportunities available. You may also meet and talk to some professionals to get an idea of that particular trade.

Fundamentals of a Career

First let us understand what we mean by being a professional. A professional enjoys intellectual engagement in a specialized job of his/her liking. He/she goes on to acquire knowledge, expertise and training in it. To be an engineer, architect, doctor, dentist, photographer, advocate, computer engineer, scientist or an accountant are some of the examples. They can be employed by institutions, the government or they can also choose to work independently. A professional is expected to work according to ethical norms of his profession. They also have to maintain integrity which means honesty, being true to those whom they work for. They also need to update themselves periodically in knowledge and skill to maintain a high standard of expertise during their career. Most of them have a decent income and respect.

My first posting in government service was in the sub divisional hospital, Khagaria (Bihar). In 1969, a seriously injured patient was admitted with multiple fractures. The most dangerous of them was of skull which led to hemorrhage inside it with compression of the brain. This resulted in coma and paralysis of one half of the body. This complication could have resulted in his death any time. He needed an urgent operation. While giving him the first aid for his fractures, I told the relatives to transport him as soon as possible to the medical college at Patna or Darbhanga. This meant a journey of 3–4 hours on a road. The patient's mother and three brothers, who were poor, went into a huddle to decide what to do.

It was a gloomy situation. On the one hand, there was the risk of operation on a critically ill patient with no alternative, and on the other, hospital was ill equipped and the doctor, young and inexperienced. After a while, one of the brothers came to me and said, 'My mother has conveyed a message to you. She has asked you to go ahead with the operation, we will accept whatever the result is, inshallah!'

Now the ball was in my court. I consulted the book on emergency surgery to refresh my memory and operated upon him. The patient responded soon on the operation table by moving his limbs. Ultimately, his recovery was complete and later walked out of the hospital.

It had left a lasting message. A professional should not avoid his duty even if the outcome does not appear favourable.

One chooses a career or job or profession to meet the basic requirements of life, like food, clothing, shelter, security, etc. to become an independent adult. Therefore, a reasonable income is a must in all employments.

It also gives one a status and respect in society. It encourages one to pursue the work with efficiency, energy, interest and satisfaction. It is a means to provide for the family. A comfortable life facilitates, to do good work for the society. This apparently simplistic explanation has other aspects which are considered later. One needs to search the rapidly growing new avenues. Artificial or Machine Intelligence is one of the many in the cutting edge. Here is a short introduction—

A.I or M.I is a device which can perceive an environment and takes appropriate action to fulfill its requirement. It functions as our brain's cognition, learning and problem-solving faculties do. The machine is available and is called Robot. It can do some of the work in industry, shop, surgical or in domestic settings. It was conceived in 1958 but this field has gained momentum in the last decade only.

Factors Which Influence Choice

The important issue of selecting a profession, business or job/employment/a means to earn should be done in a planned manner. At the outset, see which one of the three, namely, Arts, Science or Commerce suits your talent and abilities.

Then, a natural liking for a particular subject more than any other subject must be recognised. It leads a student to a particular branch of knowledge. For example, engineering and such other subjects are based on Mathematics. If one has a preference for Mathematics, logically, he can perform better in related groups of occupation. The liking or interest helps because he can acquire knowledge of the subject with relative ease. He also won't feel bored doing it day after day. He can become an expert in it in future.

The Categories of Occupation

All vocations are a source of income and other benefits. They also serve society directly or indirectly. They can present some barriers or drawbacks which may not be acceptable to all. One has to weigh the pros and cons of any profession and choose the one that is most agreeable. The professions of a chartered accountant or a doctor for example are in great demand by the aspirants because of comfortable income and respect. Such services however invite tougher competition and take longer to qualify.

❖ In any occupation it is better to find out if there is a better prospect of going higher up on the ladder with respect to income, job security and position in the workplace. If somebody has a training certificate or a diploma, he has to remain satisfied with a limited income or lower rank to begin with. The latter, generally, are easier to get because of a relatively favourable ratio of supply over demand. He has an option to upgrade his qualifications later if he is keen to upgrade himself. Many other suitable occupations exist and should be considered. A final decision depends on how much you like the job, capability and circumstances. Other factors are income, position, respect, responsibility, risk, demand, security and perquisites. However, one is sometimes compelled to take up a job which is not of his choice.

The Final choice

The related factors may be divided into two broad groups—personal inclination and practical issues.

1. *Personal inclination*:

- If one feels passionate about a particular occupation then it becomes the first choice like music, mathematics, literature or defense, technical or science related subjects.
- For independence in the workplace, one may consider business, law or medical profession. The last two can also provide regular jobs with a fixed income range.
- For a regular routine life: an administrative post in government or public undertakings or in self-employed business or academia is suitable.

- For different branches of engineering, computer hardware, software, finance or banking, science, mathematical subjects will help.
- A knack for working with people (social skill) will help them in hospital services and offices dealing with public life.
- A liking for biology is suitable for agriculture, environmental studies, medical, dental, veterinary sciences, horticulture, genetics, the pharmaceutical industry, renewable energy or water conservation.
- Aim high so that you have to work hard to achieve it. This will raise your level of application and intellect during preparation of examinations.
- If undecided, you can take an aptitude test. It is psychometric test done by a trained counselor or psychologist. They can find out about your talent and interest in a particular subject and will suggest occupation suitable to you.

This test may help the students who are either good or average in all the subjects but are unable to decide on a career.

2. *Practical issues*: The ground situation has to be considered.

- Ideally, it should be aligned to your liking and interest. The teachers at school can help because they know your temperament and ability.
- Consider what the family and well-wishers say. They can give practical solutions as they know your temperament, experience and have the means to support you.

- How long can you afford to study to prepare for competitive examinations? It is a question one should ask. You can get education loans on interest from banks payable after one is employed.

- Whether you intend to do research. For this to happen, you have to be qualified to a level of excellence in that subject. You may have to study for an extended period. The remuneration in research-based jobs is generally low compared to other professionals. However, it gives a sense of fulfillment that nothing else can.

- A new and emerging area of study may be worth a search on the internet. First you need a degree of graduation in the mother subject.

- Want to stay at one place? Any non-transferable job in a private concern or business or self-employment are such avenues. Such jobs are, however, neither well paid nor interesting.

- You can dream of doing some creative work in the profession to break the monotony. It may be about introducing a new method to get the same result, an innovation, extending the business to newer shores. The occupation should be capable to provide you a decent standard of living including healthcare and savings for security. There should be prospect of promotion further education and learning skills within the system.

- Websites can also guide you. Here are some: 'live career' or 'oprah.com', etc. A search in the internet will name many more such websites to help you in different subjects.

- You have to go through this list carefully time and again and acquire the required skills and qualifications for the most desired subject or profession in focus.

- Finally, write your career choice down in your diary, commit daily and diligently prepare to qualify for them.

- Some people are inspired to take up a subject right from their young days. This has been seen more often in the field of classical music. The famous Kumar Gandharva, a vocalist in Indian classical music, and W.A. Mozart, a composer and virtuoso in piano, western classical music, are revered names. Both enthralled their audiences before they were five years old with songs and piano respectively.

- Many scientists, mathematicians, politicians, sports persons and others in different fields decide upon a career at an early age. If you have any such feelings, it is better to choose your subject early.

- There are so many who fail to get a profession of their choice. Abraham Lincoln had faced several failures. Newton has said that success is 1 percent inspiration and 99 percent perspiration.

Basics of success

Naghma Siddiqui, a life coach, has summarized it all in an article in *The Times of India* (Speaking Tree), suggesting a three-point formula for success. This can also be applied in choosing a career. They are:

1. *Realistic attitude:* which will help you keep your feet firmly on the ground in every situation. One should not be blown away by daydreaming alone. A soaring ambition while desirable should be within your reach of hard work, intelligence and ability.

2. *Patience:* one does not always know how close one actually is to the cherished goal till one succeeds. So, the mantra is to keep going, overcoming the obstacles in the way.

3. *Self-confidence:* an inner strength of positivity after weighing your abilities against the task ahead. An intelligent approach and passion can motivate to keep you on the track in spite of failures.

Mind Map 5: WHY DO YOU NEED A CAREER?

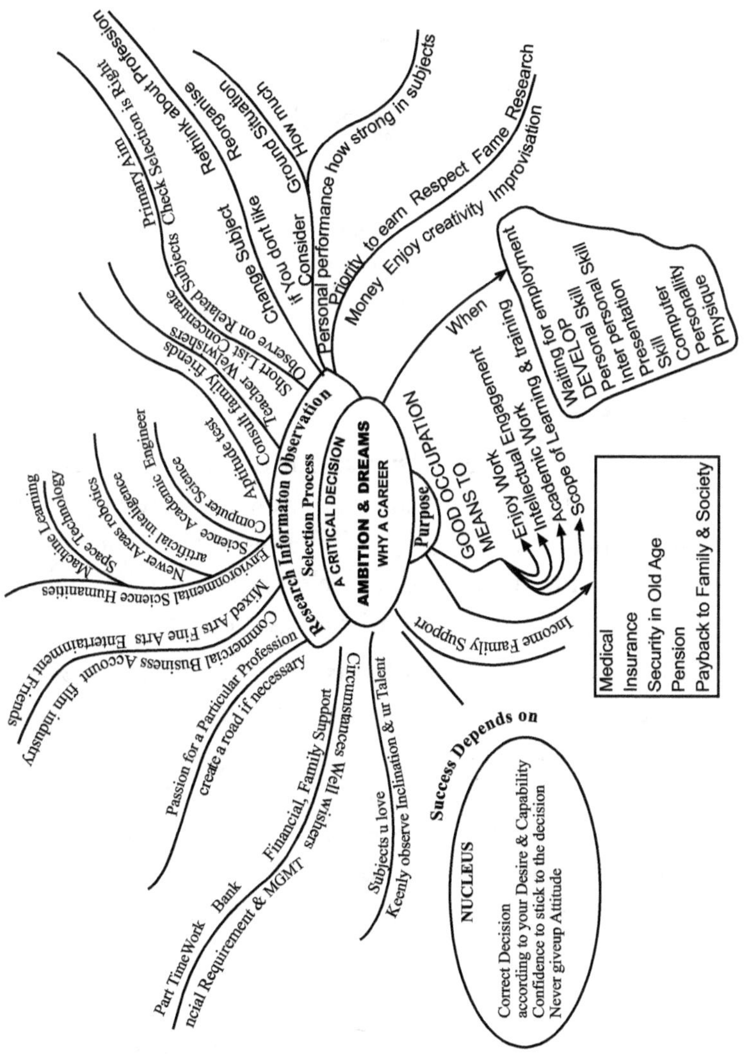

6

MEMORY

Definition

Memory is a stored representation of our sensory experience. We receive the experience through vision, hearing, smell, taste, touch and feeling. Any of the special sensory stimulations produces electrical impulses which are recorded as a trace in our brain as memory.

Your intelligence decides as to which information is important and goes on to preserve it in memory. There are millions of unwanted perceptions which need to be filtered out every second (*Need to Know NLP* by Carolyn Boyce, 2006). Memory is a primary faculty without which not only study but life itself will become unsustainable.

Types

Memory is of two types—short term and long term.

1. Short Term: It assists us in our everyday activities. A new telephone number of more than seven digits is difficult to remember for more than 10 minutes or so unless you take extra care like repeating it. This important ability keeps the data in mind till we finish the task.

2. *Long Term:* By repeating the information at intervals will convert short term memory into long term. It helps us in studies, examination, career and life in general. Proper way to study a lesson is to read its contents according to a system first and then review it regularly at intervals. Only then, it will stay in your long-term memory for months or years and enable you to recall it after long intervals.

However, you don't have to worry about memory. All normal people have equal share of this faculty. It can be improved to a great extent by anyone who regularly exercises it. By repeating a task several times, the nerve cells of the brain connect with its neighbouring nerve cells to make a network called neuroplasticity. It is like a group of friends holding another friend's hand one after the other to form a chain. Thus, a network or a path in the brain is established to pass information. For example, if one of you press the right finger of your friend on your left side and this is repeated by the latter and so on to other friends, the messaging will be transmitted on to the last friend in the chain. Repeating this many times helps to create the shortest path from the first to the last cell. (*Train Your Brain* by Ryuta Kawashima, 2016). By using this pathway of message repeatedly, the connection becomes strong, lasting and makes passage of message quicker.

Chemistry of Memory

All information we receive, undergo the steps of perception and internal processing to be stored as memory. We use this memory as and when required in written, verbal or in the form of body language.

1. *Perception* is the first impression we register through our senses. Attention applied solely to this perception with emotional engagement facilitates registration further. Attention is the first among all other faculties of students.

2. *Internal* processing is to understand the information and then arrange the data systematically. An intelligent and orderly placement of these data in the mind makes recollection easy.

Mnemonics: The tools which modify information for its easy recall are called mnemonics. There are several ways to make it. The most useful of them are in written form like mind map or acronym or short poem by using contents of the matter to make it memory-friendly. In fact, remembering the number of days in a month (in a year) is made easier by this example—there are 30 days in November, April June and September. Again, the key to remember is only review, review and review. It makes the neural pathway a lasting highway.

Associating any data or concept with what you already know, like place or articles, idea or names is called *pegging*. It is a great help to remember this way. Some children have this sense aplenty. You too can easily develop it. A child when asked to describe a zebra said, 'It is a striped horse,' and another when asked about a lichi said, 'It is like a *rasgulla,* with a cockroach in its stomach!'

The first letter of several pieces of data can be joined together to form an Acronym. BMETR is a product of this effort.

The first six alphabets of English can be used to remember the tools. A is Acronym and Association (Attachment or Pegging). B is to Break a list of a large data into smaller manageable bits according to their quality, number or other features and group them. C is to create or compare: mnemonics like mind map and notes are creations. A statement, story or concept can be compared to another about their character, equality, nature, utility or any other quality to help remember it. D is to draw a diagram or graph, E is edit to discard the unimportant and retain what is important in what you study. F is to filter in the funnel of HW formula, namely—how, who, where, what, etc. It has got wide applicability.

2. *External processing* (output) is done after you have absorbed the material internally. It can be done in written, verbal or in silent form with sign and body language (dance or gestures). It consolidates the memory further. Verbal is expression in the form of speech, presentation, lecture or discussion. A written document is meant for periodical review to keep it in long term memory. These include making Mind maps, Notes and flash cards diagrams etc. Verbal reviews are recitation and group discussion. Examples of silent review are Manan and Nididhyasan (a type of contemplation or dhyana when the material needs to be absorbed).

A study system like SQ3R study i.e., Question, read, revise and review (www.niagraeduoaas) is a good example of combining the 3 steps of perception, Internal and external processing.

Memory is used like a rope (or thread) to learn or express. If one end is pulled, the rest of the rope comes in your hand because of its continuity. For convenience, you put knots at intervals in the form of headings, sub heading and key words as landmarks (knots) to remind yourself of the entire connected study material which will be easier to recall and express.

Examples of Memory Power

There are instances of some gifted people with amazing memory power. Once, in India, some British soldiers were bathing in the Ganges. Two of them quarrelled and traded punches. This led to a court case and summoning of Indians who had witnessed the fight. All the Indians expressed their inability to repeat the words exchanged as they did not know the English language. Only one elderly person volunteered to say what had happened. However, he too was ignorant of English language but could reproduce what went on verbally between the two. He was, in fact, known for his excellent memory in the locality. The judge understood and recorded his statement in English. The complainants confirmed it. The satisfied judge finally gave his verdict based on it.

There are many instances of stupendous memory feats through the ages. Even now, there are scholars who can recite the whole Quran, Bible or Mahabharata without aid of books.

In vedic times, young gurukul students used to memorise the Vedas by *Shravana,* i.e., by listening to the teachings of the guru followed by *manana* and *nididhyasana.* There was no script or books in olden times. You can also try to remember a classroom lecture you hear. But for that, you need to apply the two steps—careful listening and internal processing (store in orderly way: *manana*). Then, finally, make a note of it after the lecture is over. You may further refer to <ajitvadakayil.blogspot.in/2014/101shravana mananidinidhyasana-way-of.html> and <ajitvadakayil.blogspot.com> which explains it accurately.

Shravana means listening with attention and digesting it. It is at the sensory level with intensely registering the data received. While listening (or for that matter doing any job), attention has a natural tendency to jump to any other object like a monkey. To keep attention fixed to a single object of your interest, you have to pull your attention back to the first object. This repeated effort is known as *Pratyahara*. Exercise it daily and then the interrupted attention gets converted from a drop-by-drop status to a continuous and lasting flow of thick oil from a drum.

Manana is reflecting on the content imbibed by *shravana*. Doubts are raised and explained with appropriate logic by a teacher or by participants as in group discussion. It was a method in ancient India to investigate truth behind a concept or hypothesis. It leads to a crystal-clear perception about the subject under discussion. This is review done by yourself at the processing level.

Nididhyasana is deep contemplation on the subject till one understands it totally. One can then discover its new meaning or implications. This can lead to a new concept or hypothesis by adding new ideas to it. *Nididhyasana* is largely at the processing level (brain storming individually) till a conclusion is reached.

Principles of Memory Exercise

They are essentially based on recollection and repetition. By physical exercise, the muscles become powerful. Similarly, if you study daily, solve mathematical or other problems repeatedly, your brain becomes sharper. Also, from good deeds by helping the needy, you become emotionally resilient. Follow a daily routine and you will become a disciplined and punctual person. This is a law of nature. Some of the methods to exercise memory are mentioned in other chapters. With a good memory one can express the substance of any topic effortlessly like a copy-and-paste click of a computer. After all, each nerve cell of the brain is a computer with intelligence.

- Brain can register one information only at a time. Numerous other useless data which come to our senses are filtered out consciously or subconsciously. It pays attention to only that which the brain selects.

- Joshua Foer (2012) in his book 'Moon Walking with Einstein ' has elaborated on the ancient Roman way (Loci system) of remembering a list of items or facts or images. The principle is to store these items you want to recall later, in different rooms of a building, home or space, which you are familiar with. It is important that you pay full attention to the items and the location, building or space while storing it. It will help if you visualize the object to be recalled and the location vividly time and again.

- *Trataka* is an aid to enhance concentration. Physical exercise makes muscles and bones stronger. Daily study and solving mathematical problems improve our intelligence. Selfless service enriches our compassion. Giving importance to time saves time. A regular routine can balance our life. Likewise repeated use of the faculty of our memory will empower our memory. The neurones, too, like the muscle fibres obey the rule of exercise. They increase their neuroplasticity and remain active and strong lifelong.

- Pet Scan studies (A radiological picture of physiolologicallyactiveareas) of brainhave revealed that with intensive study and learning, the area dealing with memory, namely Hippocampus, increases in size (*The Sharp Brains Guide to Brain Fitness*; page 28–29; 2013).

- Developing a sense of enquiry and wonder and by using W-H formula with a will to remember, helps to memorize.

- One can memorize selected important lessons to score marks like nothing else can.

- The four friends of study are attention, interest, sense of wonder and satisfaction of achieving something.

- In the commitment page to be read in the golden hour of routine, you can always add fresh commitments from time to time..

- All information is received by the special senses. As a student, vision hearing and using spatial sense are more important for study. By engaging more senses, your overall cognitive intelligence improves.

- A mind map in colour is thus superior to note-taking.

- Emotionally likable matter or subject is easier to remember.

- A video of a place is good. However, a personal visit can make you remember it better because you have seen it in three dimensions and experienced and enjoyed the scenery (an element of feeling).

- A *gulab jamun* is best remembered by tasting it. But if a ruffian tries to snatch it, you will eat it in a hurry. The *gulab jamun* then will not taste as delicious. Stress spoils our mindfulness in what we see, feel or do. It affects our memory and studies.

While we discuss the exercise of long-term memory in details in the next chapter, let us have a look at the exercises of short-term memory below.

Exercise of Short-Term Memory (or working memory)

Let us play with it though we unknowingly use it every day. The calculation is done by memory of tables or mentally. In the latter, we hold the numbers in mind (memory) and complete the steps to get the result. Multiply 15 with 35 mentally. You can multiply without the help of table. Mentally calculate the numbers and get 525. It requires to hold the numbers in your mental eye as you multiply 35 with 5 first and then with 1 and keep the figures in the mind's eye to add. You can improvise and play with increasing numbers—adding, subtracting or dividing, all mentally—to improve short-term memory. This was numerical example. We use short-term memory very often when we talk or discuss or do any work physically or mentally. We have to remember what we have said or done and what we will speak or do next. Doing exercises with numbers or words is always fun.

Zera Colburn, a genius once calculated mentally the numbers of minutes and seconds in a span 48 years' period and gave the correct answers as 25,228,800 and 151,3 72,800 respectively. In India, Shakuntala Devi and

Ramanujan were also well known for their mathematical wizardry. They all had one thing in common—stupendous short-term memory.

You can recall facts of everyday life. For example, what you ate in breakfast, lunch, dinner, etc. in the last 24 hours. Next, try to find out the menu of a day before and so on in the past. You can try the same regarding the dress of friends, the landmarks on the way or what was the routine about two or three days back, on your way to school. You can try to remember faces of important people. If you are right-handed, then try to use left hand increasingly more or vice versa. Try to solve puzzles, crossword, Sudoku or spellathon. You can make a habit to dive into waters of yesterday's activities. You may not find a pearl but will improve memory power in the long run. These are all examples of challenging (exercising) the brain which increases our cognitive intelligence.

Make a dull subject interesting

Sometimes, for no valid reason, you dislike a subject. It may be Arithmetic, History or even Biology. You avoid studying the related book and get poor marks as a result. This further discourages you. This may force you to go for a career which has very little use of that villain of a subject. This may deprive you of a good choice. Let us find out the cause. Actually, all subjects are logical and interesting. Moreover, they serve an important purpose. Otherwise they would not exist. They are based on concepts. Concept is a general principle or model which has been proved correct time and again. Their application leads to profitable solutions. For example, fire can alter the physical and chemical state of an object or a living being because of its high temperature. It has been proved by cooking vegetables. The reason why you do not like a subject is because you may not have understood its concept. Once you understand the concept or idea behind a subject, you will develop a liking for it. If you are unable to appreciate it, a teacher can explain it to you. I am sure once you get hold of the concept, you will like the subject.

Study and Memory

Kevin Paul in his book, *Study Harder, Not Smarter,* 2013, in page 58, has quoted Ebbinghaus' experiment. It has proved that to remember a study material, you have to actively study and without delay you have to actively remember it by review. If you fail to do so, it gradually fades away.

How memory and study are related?: Good memory is the ability to retain and reproduce it later—whatever you have studied. This helps to secure good marks. You can always improve this ability with effort. So, cultivate it with all your might as suggested below.

SQ3R is a practical example of this concept. To see, hear and feel are important in that order in order to capture any information in your memory. A visit to a beautiful place stays in memory longer than watching a video of the same. Mr. Paul has advised to involve all the seven intelligences and five special senses while reading whenever possible. For example, reading aloud takes the help of visual, auditory and feelings and is more effective to retain. Group discussion helps in the growth of interpersonal skills. By using graphics and colours in Mind Map, adding tune to poetry, rhyme or mnemonic helps.

A variety of sensation coming regularly will leave a lasting memory trace on brain. A liking for what you study is a big positive emotional factor. You have to be mindful and enjoy it to welcome it in memory.

Find out if you can draw a chart or map or any other data you have seen in a text book. You can also draw anything else with memory. Visual and spatial memory is our strength. You can make it stronger by practise. Strengthening visual memory can be done on your way to school or any other place as a pastime. Try to remember places, houses or buildings or river, sea or hills you have seen. The more you exercise your faculties, better it would be.

How to Do Well in Examination

You might be thinking that why is it that we all cannot excel in studies? What is the problem? Science indicates that we all can, unless mentally deficient. Please accept the fact that by and large we all are normal persons with similar potential in memory and intelligence. We can have as much knowledge as those who get high marks and are in the top ten.

It actually is the burning desire within them to do better in the examinations. This resolve inspires them to readily recall knowledge, ability to write legibly and systematically and, more importantly, keep calm and focused in examination hall. In order to gather knowledge, you need to study well enough to cover the entire syllabus. We aim to know everything about the important chapters and something of the not-so-important ones. The biggest hurdle for most of us is that we consider study as hard work. Anything which we don't like becomes hard for us.

Playing a favourite game in the field or any other pastime makes us so happy and energetic. This sadly is not the case with study, usually. What is the reason?

It is because we fail to apply the mixed factors of inquisitiveness (interest), love of application (attachment) wonder (joy), and at the end, a sense of achievement (you have done your best) to study. These very four good feelings generate energy to play and continue it for long. These four can be applied to study as well. In study, we search to find the whole truth of a lesson applying the same four feelings. A toddler who fiddles with a new toy, a girl who learns to cycle in spite of fall or hurt and kids enjoying games to the point of exhaustion are all driven by above four factors. Then why not study? One who wants to do well in anything has to develop this mixed bag of four on the mantra of 'More you exercise, stronger it becomes'. This second factor of exercise is there in us (See Chapter 3) too. It is waiting to get a break and a chance.

A game is interesting because there is competition involved between opposing players or teams. The physical activity, role of intelligence, fitness, the two warring teams changing tactics every moment, etc. are things that absorb us. They keep changing their aggression and defence, and finally face the glorious suspense as to who will win at the final whistle. One can treat study as a sport. It has got the same four factors of desire to know—interest (inquisitiveness), application (involvement), wonder (joy) and, at the end, to feel good that you have done your best (achievement). There is no room for blaming others, including luck in play or study. Your involvement with such sportsman spirit matters the most.

To be good at football, you must have a strong desire to be an ace footballer. You have to take a few hundred shots to be a good scorer. In the beginning, it is difficult because brain cells have to respond to different set of obstructions in neural pathway. By trial and error, it finds a blueprint to score goals. It is like going to a new place. You may take a longer path on first attempt to reach it. It is only after multiple visits to the area and by trial-and-error method, those brain cells get connected by the shortest route. After using the shortest neural path several times, you will find it easy to score goals like Messi or Ronaldo. It is like when you master cycling, you can sing and talk and pass through very narrow lanes or busy traffic. Same is the case when you study with above-mentioned four factors repeatedly. At the end, practice, practice and practice is the key.

So read every day, solve arithmetic sums or problems many a times. Then, regularly review to remember them. Regular study nurtures your faculty of memory. This is a formidable combination for success.

Sue Dunkle (2011) <https://www.ucg.org/user/sue-dunkle> and a blog (2017) <https://wwwfloridacaree college.edu/blog/common-traits-of-highly-successful-students>

World champion P. Sindhu (Olympic silver medallist) starts training badminton at 4.30 AM everyday and has been doing it for the last 12 years. Wonder gymnast Dipika did one thousand times 'Produnova', a dangerous gymnastic vault, in three months prior to Olympics. Think of their passion to perform in their games. That is what will inspire us and the generations to come!

Mind Map 6: WHAT IS MEMORY?

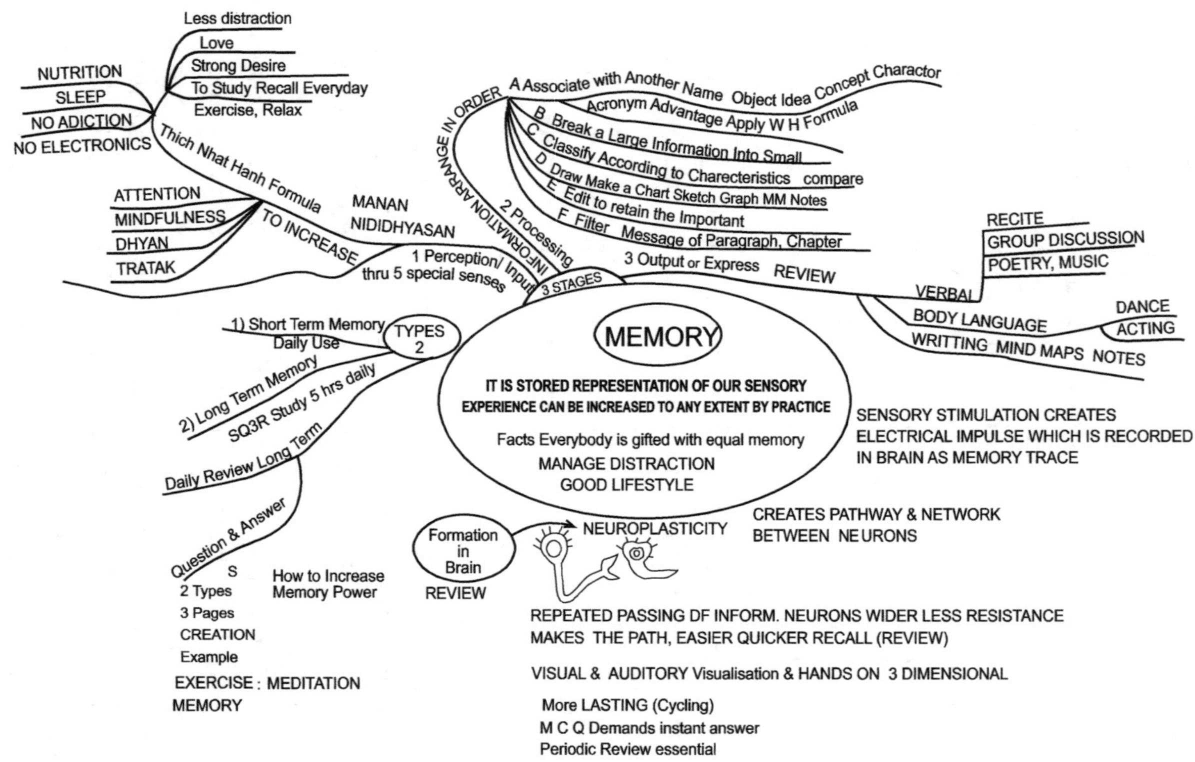

<u>7</u>

THE WAY TO STUDY

Study is an interesting responsibility and certainly the only means to achieve what you want in life. It enables you to acquire knowledge and skill to qualify in class or competitive examination. Aim of study is to secure them in long-term memory and easy recollection of the same.

Factors Which Matter

Attention or mindfulness, concentration, love for the subject and will are factors which matter.

Attention is the ability to be aware of what you think, speak or do in the present time excluding everything else. It is the first and most important factor for effective study. The challenge is whether you are capable of collecting your attention by warding off the distractions repeatedly. One can do it with detachment and practice.

Concentration is the ability to keep the attention undisturbed over an extended period of time. This can be compared to the uninterrupted flow of oil when it is poured from a bottle.

Trataka is a tool to increase concentration. Paste a small black dot or mark on the wall at an arm's length, level with your eyes. Sit on a chair or on the floor in *asana* posture. Sit still with straight back and gaze mindfully on the spot. Gradually, increase the duration from 5 to 15 minutes in 2–3 weeks.

Review and *memory* aids are intelligent ways to store it for a long term.

Emotion along with *determination* and *love* to retain the important task permanently, is the key.

Study can also be an interesting pastime or a challenge to test how much you remember after sometime. To think that you have studied for five hours as per routine and that your responsibility is over will not be of much help.

After you qualify and enter a profession, you may have to learn a new subject or skill. To learn how to learn is a prized skill. In pursuit of this, research has been carried out worldwide. In *Study Smarter Not Harder* (2013) by Kevin Paul there are many of his and other authors' suggestions given for our benefit.

Stages of Study and Preparation

Study has three stages—pre-study preparation, the act of study and, lastly, post-study follow up. Each of these is an indispensable part of effective study.

1. Pre-study Preparation: It aims to make your surroundings quiet to help absorb what you study.

Distractions can be external or internal and both have to be kept to a minimum level.

External Distractions

The study room has to be kept free of distractions like music, television, radio, people talking or passing by, mobiles, pets and insects like mosquitoes or flies. Use mosquito nets or insect repellent if necessary. A quiet room helps us to concentrate. On the other hand, it has also been seen that a truly interested pupil can study effectively under a street lamp or in a bazaar or even by the side of a busy railway station. So, paying attention to a task with mindfulness excluding all else is a difficult but necessary exercise.

A serious student should be prepared to forego activities which are likely to interfere with studies especially before examination. Games like football, hockey, cricket matches could be tiring and time consuming. If at all, play for a limited time to stay fresh for study later. Telly serials, social mobile calls, a get-together, parties, cinema and political debates are distracting activities. It is better to avoid them totally. Such activities may interfere with study and sleep, thereby, affecting the routine of next day.

In 1960-61, I was working at Patna Medical College Hospital as a house surgeon in a busy surgical unit. I was kept engaged daily from 8 AM to 8 PM and on Sundays and during weekly emergencies. The workload was quite heavy. One day, I was busy in assisting with an operation when I was called for an emergency at around 5 PM. It was an unconscious and restless patient with head injury. As he had to undergo an X-ray examination,

I advised a morphine injection for him along with other instructions. I returned to the operation theatre only to realise that I had made a blunder by prescribing morphine, which was contraindicated in head injury cases. I informed my chief immediately. Furious, he enquired how could I prescribe morphine in such a case. I kept silent.

My chief and I rushed to the emergency, but by that time the injection was already given. He was then advised a few more injections, oxygen and other measures, including an antidote for morphine by my chief, but unfortunately the antidote was not available. Even after all life saving measures were taken, the patient could not be saved. I spent many days in remorse, cursing myself for such an expensive mistake. I realised that a decision taken when one is physically and mentally tired or stressed, often turns wrong. Now, I refrain from taking any major decision when I am not in a normal state. It is better to take rest before getting too tired. Tread on the path of truth. Setbacks are only temporary events on the sand dunes of time.

Venue (place): All work and no play makes you a dull girl/ boy. It is good to enjoy games and entertainment but not more than 2–3 hours a day.

To study, sit with a straight back on a comfortable chair, at a table with your feet on the floor. All books and papers should be within your hand's reach. There should be minimum body movement during study as in a *yogasana*. An adjustable table lamp and another light if available from behind can be soothing to the eyes. Wear comfortable clothes.

If you study on the floor, sit with your legs crossed or in *vajrasana* (See chapter on Routine) with a straight back. The reading material can be kept supported at a distance of about 10 inches or so from your eyes.

It is wise to take a break for ten minutes after an hour of study. Study not more than two hours in one session and one subject for no more than 1 hour at a time. After each session of two hours, take a longer break.

If some stray thoughts disturb you or if the mind wanders, apply *ThitchNhat Hanh* formula or advice. He emphasises to be aware of our breath,thought, word and deed every moment. So, when you study, resolve: The fact that I am studying is a great feeling. I am being myself completely. I am conscious of my breath, my presence, my posture and immersed in what I am studying. No power on this earth can disturb me.

If unwanted thoughts come, passively wait and watch them fade away. Do not be occupied with them. It will disappear like a breakaway kite. Breathe mindfully for 2–3 minutes to get back your attention.

The great Indian mathematician, Ramanujan, was on a balcony in London when the Queen's Coronation procession was passing underneath. Later, when asked how much he had enjoyed it, he had replied that he heard nothing of the noise or din of the marching military bands play. Ramanujan was at that time lost in his mathematical world, playing with numbers.

Internal Distraction

It is important to have a tranquil mind. Early in the morning after the golden hour of exercise you are fresh mentally and physically. Then your mind is alert and receptive, it is the time to study. Distraction is minimised by:

- Doing all work and activities including study, play, eating and interacting, mindfully day long.
- Following the routine and commitments made during golden hour.

If you are still distracted

- Sit in your study room.

- Ignore old problems.

- Do some breathing exercises or meditate or just do simple one-digit calculations.

- Think of the students who are studying all over the world, take inspiration from them. Wish them happiness.

- Soon, you will get back your concentration and alpha brain wave to help you study.

A Way to Study (SQ3R Method)

It is better to study following a plan or system. One good system is called SQ3R.

The objective is to understand what you study and recall the matter later when required, e.g., in the examination hall. First try to remember what you already know about the chapter, fit it into what you are studying and keep the combined facts under proper headings, subheadings and keywords. It is a step-by-step method to get the whole material into your long-term memory.

The SQ3R system is: Survey, Question, Read (1) Recite (2) (speak out loudly what you have read), and Review (3) (preparing a review tool is making a note or mind map). Review material is a valuable document which is used regularly throughout the year as an aid to recall and revise a particular task.

The system keeps you interested and busy with the study material which helps you to remember.

SURVEY (S):

You get a general idea of the book by noting the title of the book and list of contents. While reading a chapter, remember headings, subheadings, tables, graphs and other illustrations. Also go through the first and last paragraph of the chapter for the message author wants to convey. Note the keywords of each paragraph diligently. These key words are the connecting links of message of each paragraph. While you survey, keep asking Questions of WH formula simultaneously. The survey is to get a general idea of the matter and takes a few minutes extra with practice.

QUESTION (Q):

While you survey till you finish reading the chapter (S,R1,R2), keep asking questions about each sentence. Write the questions that you have framed yourself. It will clarify whether the text answers all the questions you have asked.

READ (R1):

It is to understand the contents in details and to get the answers of your questions. Note the important milestone or keywords of each paragraph. They will help you to remember the content. Then connect the keywords to know the theme of all paragraphs. Thus, you will comprehend the whole chapter. Go through the process of R1 slowly and attentively.

RECITE (R2):

Recite verbally and audibly to listen what you have grasped. If in doubt, clarify it by opening the text again. This is an age-old proven way to memorise important information. It combines senses like reading (vision), auto listening (hearing) and feeling (kinaesthetic). 95 per cent of information comes through eyes and ears in human beings.

Repeating a few times will keep the material in your long-term memory. The number tables or poems memorised in this way also stays lifelong. It can be done for a few limited important chapters.

REVIEW (R3):

Review can be:

1. Written: Mind map, notes, flashcard
2. Mental: *smaran, manan, nididhyaasan*
3. Verbal: Group study

Review Making and Its Use

Review has two sides like that of a coin. First is to give a shape to the chapter, such as by mind mapping. The other side is its use at regular intervals (to do review) to remember it longer. Important chapters of all subjects can be earmarked at the beginning of each semester for review.

The first side of tool making—mind map (MM), note (N) and flashcards are best made within 30 minutes or as soon as practicable. Consult the chapter again to confirm that all important points have been included. They need to be neatly recorded in a durable, long, unruled exercise book in block letters legibly. Make sure that it represents all the important aspects of a chapter (covering the heading, subheading, keywords, tables and illustrations) in short but has enough points (keywords) to lead you to recapitulate the important contents of the chapter.

Second side—is to practise the R3 (review) document (MM or Notes). First try to recall mentally the MM or notes, and then, with the help of the keywords, try to remember the content of the chapter. This is exercised regularly to help recall the content of the chapter till examination. Doing an R3 gets gradually shorter with time. It is vital to review regularly and recall the connecting details of linking the headings, subheadings, keywords, diagrams, mnemonics or questions. First, try to recall without consulting the R3 instrument and then open it to find out what you have missed. Next time, try to remember it all. The details of R3-making (under a time table) is discussed later.

SQ3R is designed to let you have an outline of the book and chapter and to understand what it is all about (S). Then you study the material closely to understand it (R1). Interest is kept alive by asking questions (Q), then you apply WH formula, as you read through it (R1). Then recite audibly for long term memory (R2). Thus S, Q and

R1 and R2 all go together. If repeated every day for a few days it can be memorised verbatim. This over learning is reserved only for formulae, arithmetic tables, poems, scientific laws, Sanskrit and classifications.

Lastly but importantly, for long term benefit of SQ3R system is the periodic review of R3 with the help of mind maps (MM), notes (N) and *shrawan, manan,* etc. Doing R3 extensively a few weeks prior to examination with these notes or MM will enable you to revise all chapters of subjects in a short time. Notes or MM is essential for at least all the important topics. No study is complete without making R3 and no preparation is good enough without regular exercising R3, i.e., doing the review. Repetition is the key to remember anything and SQ3R is an intelligent device to do it.

Please note:

- Study a subject for no more than an hour or so at a time. It is usually enough to complete all the steps of SQ3R. With practice it will become a habit, easier and faster. Take a break for 10 minutes. Then you can take up another different subject as per your preference for an hour.
- If you read two chapters, one by SQ3R method and another by the old method, you can feel the difference between the two.
- Please make sure to read all important material adopting this system. It might appear burdensome at first but it will eventually get comfortable with practise.
- Critical listening in the class lecture. Try to remember the headings, subheadings their gist of

content message, data, numbers, graphs and tables. Do not worry if you miss some of them. You can always recall it later. Keep thinking at the end about the new things you have learnt and its significance. Aim is to note the points only to make a proper MM or N soon after the class. This habit will enable you to retain more and more.

Post Study Follow up

Review of a chapter takes five to ten minutes. Repeat it first every day for a week and then weekly for a month, then monthly every three months till examination.

With regular review, the entire subject will be clear in the mind's eye for the examination. With the passage of time the review material of different subjects will pile up. You then have to allot time and an exercise book copy for each subject. You also have to prepare a reminder chart to tell you when the next review is due in each subject.

The Mind Map Book by Tony and Barry Buzan (2003) has introduced some revolutionary ideas in study skills. They recommend classroom lecture can also be recorded in this form as the lecture goes on.

Technique of Making a MM (As instructed in Tony and Barry Buzan's book)

- A Mind Map is a graphic representation of the contents of a chapter on a single page with all the important data so it is memory-friendly and easier to review. You can use a pencil in the beginning.

- Heading of the chapter (theme) is written at the centre with lines radiating from it. On each radiating line you print the keywords or headings, subheadings or data in legible block letters of different sizes to accommodate them. The extended lines bear related information about subheadings, etc., encouraging connectivity.

- Use of different colours makes the different main headings or sub headings easier to remember. The completed MM tool becomes a quick and enjoyable experience. Visual memory and recall of details of the headings and keywords of the mind map stay longer than written words of Notes.

- Get a durable notebook for each subject even for mathematical formulae, etc. The graphic design generates creative thinking

By following Mantra of BMETR and practising meditation and *Trataka*, you can improve memory and concentration further. You can come out with innovative and alternate ideas on the subject you study and discover something new. Here's a true story that will inspire you—

Swami Vivekananda in the United States used to borrow a large number of books everyday from a nearby library. The very next day he would return all the books borrowed the previous day and ask for a new set of books. This puzzled the librarian. The Librarian one day asked the Swami that whether the Swami read the books at all or not. Vivekananda replied that he read all the books thoroughly and asked the librarian to take any book that he had just returned and ask questions about any one of them. She picked up a book and asked Swamiji as to what was written on a particular page. Swamiji recited the page word for word which left the librarian dumbfounded.

Group Discussion: Two or more friends of compatible temperaments can review an important chapter within a specified duration and place. All must come prepared with questions, books, mind map, MCQs. Somebody can start the session by asking a question. Everybody should ask questions and seek answer by rotation. Questions of MCQs or their difficulties should be discussed. It takes more time but you don't feel it. The practise of verbal expression and a short examination experience in a friendly atmosphere is helpful. You will remember better and feel more confident to express or face an examination after a few sessions. Here are some random measures to improve memory and easily recall things:

1. Teaching a junior is also a sort of review and is helpful.

2. Adequate sleep is vital for study.

3. Concentration is paying attention to a single task to the exclusion of all. This is the ideal way to study or doing anything efficiently.

4. It is necessary to study by yourself for five hours a day to comprehend subjects. Doing well in class tests gives confidence. If you do not get regular tests, then solve the examination papers on a regular basis

Technique of Making a Flashcard:

You can prepare such handy 4 inches by 4 inches cards to write a material in data form and abbreviations which you want to remember. You can carry them in your pocket for quick review while travelling or waiting somewhere. Broad headings, important list of names, dates, data, formulae, classification of a subject, etc. are suitable for this. One can also use old wall calendar to the same effect when at home. Nowadays, a palm top or an ipad can also be used.

Ancient Tactics:

There was no script or books in existence in ancient times. *Sravan, Manan and Nididhyasana* were the three steps practised to remember voluminous philosophical treatise and handed over from one generation to the next for many centuries in India. Practise *Shrawan* in the class with full attention. Mark the headings, key words, pose questions as in the SQ3R system while listening. Try to remember the points the teacher has described like the paragraphs in the book. Keep connecting the key words. After the class, make a note as early as possible. *Manan* (contemplation) is done at home alone as a mental review within 24 hours in a relaxed way without consulting a mind map or note. Consult a book after this is done to add anything important that you have missed. *Manan* is another convenient way to review when you have time but have no written material available. You can thus develop a sharp mind. Many good students consult the chapter taught in the class by reading it the same day in the library of school or on reaching home. *Nididhyasana* is deeper contemplation in the form of brainstorming. Probably it was meant to be a mental debate of the matter read with questions of WH (who, how, etc.) formula. You can think of the effects in different situations. It is an exercise of the imagination and alternative forms of thinking. It may help you to remember very important topics and also prepare the brain for research.

Frame MCQs yourself to be creative. Ordinary people like you and I are not as gifted as Ramanujan or Swami Vivekananda. But we can improve our memory and concentration to a great extent with regular exercise, meditation, yoga, *trataka*, *pranayama* and love for studies. We can make them a habit for life. One can adopt a combination of modern and ancient techniques of India profitably.

Sue Dunkle (2011) (https:/'www.ucg.org/user/suedunkle) has pointed out some traits found in successful students:

- It is futile to guess about the results of any examination because you cannot.
- Always ask the teacher if you fail to understand what he has said, in the class or later.
- Always study particular subjects at a scheduled hour daily.
- Fix the subjects beforehand.
- Study the difficult subjects when you are fresh.
- Never defer study till the last segment of time.
- **'Daily Review' is the common trait in all successful students.**

Some Tips by Educationists for Parents:

- Spending quality time with children daily paves a way to enable students to overcome stress, opine the psychologists.
- The pressure of studies and examination can demoralise or depress any one. One has to be alert.

A student can perform only when he/she is happy and is encouraged by the near and dear ones. So be compassionate.

- Nagging for study is often counter-productive. Students will them selves realise its importance.

- Examination is not everything after all. There is much more in life beyond it. Let them wear the coat of examination loosely.

- Students commit suicide every hour which is preventable.

- The entire family sometimes appear to be partaking in the examination.

- Abroad, and now in India, the examination results are certainly not the most important criterion for job selection.

- Jobs are economy-dependant. Students have no role in it.

- The Indian parents are held in high esteem in India and abroad. We need to let it continue even in the modern times.

Mind Map 7: THE WAYS TO STUDY

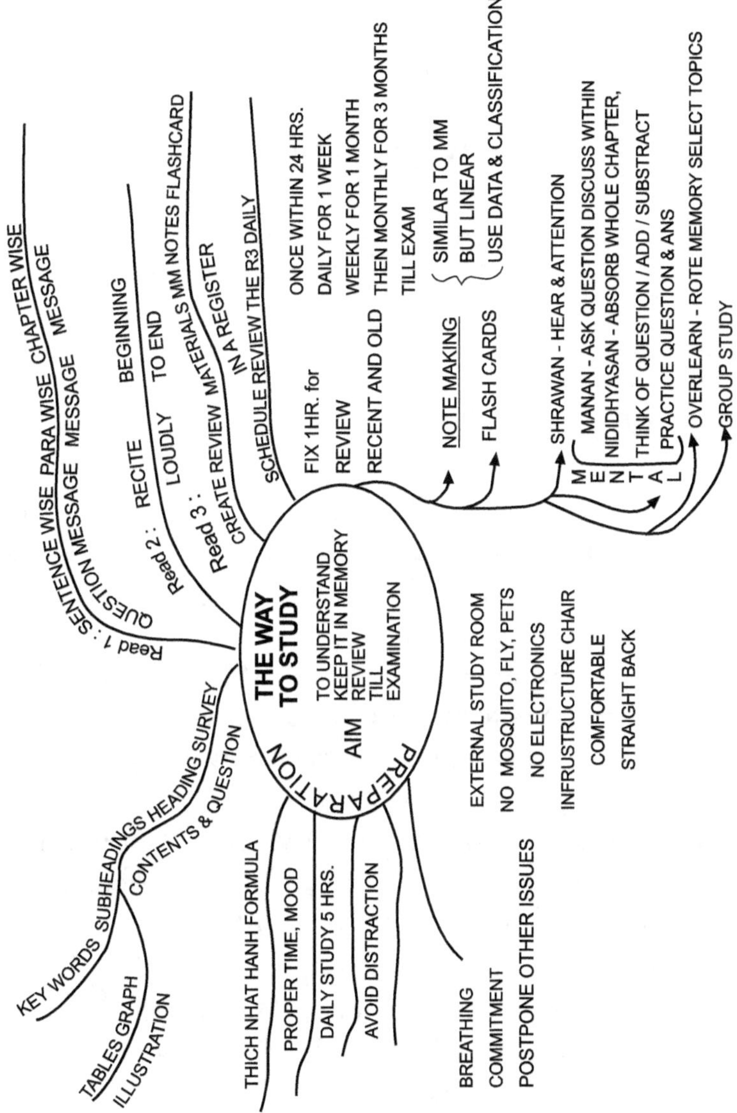

<u>8</u>

ROUTINE

Why Adopt a Routine

- To spend each day logically, timely and sequentially to help create a neural pathway in the brain, making it a habit. That will make a day long work easy and stress free.

- To ensure one hour to exercise BME in the morning, eight hours for school, allocate five hours to study, three hours for play and relaxation and seven hours for sleep.

- To ensure getting up at 5 AM, as the first morning hour is most healthy, quiet and non-interfering time to upgrade the all important BME.

- Routine minimises distraction in the waking hours.

- A sunrise oriented body clock is physiological (Circadian Rhythm)for all activities and makes it convenient for the household.

A General Outline

Action begins at 5 AM and ends at 9 PM.

The youth have an inquisitive mind with unending energy. They have hardly any worldly responsibility. So, they are in a position to utilize and enjoy every bit of the 24 hours and enrich their growing BMETR.

The golden hour of early morning from 5:30 to 6:30 is ideal to nurture body, mind and soul 24/7. This makes it imperative to wake up at 5 AM, do the morning rituals to be ready at 5:30 AM, irrespective of season.

The 24 hours is meant to provide all important 7–8 hours for sleep, 8 hours for school and 5 hours for study at home. One should equally enjoy the free 2–3 hours for personal work, games, time with friends and relaxation.

Starting the day early is considered ideal since ancient times. The majority of modern lifestyle coaches also recommend it. A student can achieve any goal in life by following the routine regularly and sincerely. In pre-examination preparation one can modify the rest of activities during the day, except the golden hour. Routine can be suspended when you are unable to follow it physically.

It is suggested to avoid mobile phones totally except in emergency or for some important reason. Please also limit watching television to one hour only once a week and cinema once a fortnight. There are undesirable side effects of use of electronic gadgets which have been reported in many researches on students globally.

The outline of the suggested routine may appear to be a bit tight at first sight. In practise, there will be enough room to compensate for study and fun by stealing some time from holidays. You are also free to allocate some bits of time to study during intervals between classes/travelling time. One has to make use of time for study during the holidays and weekends to remain up to date.

On holidays: Study two extra hours (apart from the routine of 5 hours on usual days) preferably before noon i.e., three hours in the morning, two hours each in the afternoon and evening, making it seven hours in all. Give equal importance to review in all studies. Morning session: Study 45 minutes, followed by a 15-minute review or review making of the same subject. Take a break for 10 minutes. Then again study 45 minutes, followed by a 15-minute review or review making of the same subject. Then again take a break for 10 minutes. Then do a one-hour session of only review of important chapters of other subjects. Keep a list of chapters reviewed in a register meant for it. This completes morning session of three hours.

On holidays, you may study differently if it suits you. Study three hours in the morning session and four hours in the afternoon or the other way round. One can do *Manan* and group study with the help of MM, notes or flashcards. It will give you entire evening to relax or play.

If you are going out of station on holidays for more than a few days, then take all the review notes and MM and notes copy with you. Go through them for an hour only after the golden hour or any other time available. It is a good practise to keep in touch with study daily even if for a short time.

Some schools open early in the morning. The students can take rest after coming home and, thereafter, continue their studies. They can use the commuting time to review (*Manan*). Those who come home late, can play at school or join yoga or music class there (if such facilities exist). Alternatively, they can study longer after they reach home to complete five hours' study schedule.

Mornings from 5 to 5:30: is spent in toilet, cleansing, bathing and getting ready for the day. This is also when you pray and wish well for all the students of the world.

The Golden Hour

From 5:30 to 6:30: This session is ideal for exercise of body, mind and emotion. Three sessions, 20 minutes eachare allocated for running + shavasan, asana + dhyana, and exercise of emotion and commitments respectively. Asana Pranayam Mudra Bandh (2004) which is the name of the book by Swami Satyananda Saraswati. Asana and Vipassana (Dhyana) as taught by S.K.Goenka, (2014).

First 20 minutes: running and *shavasan*.

15 minutes: Start the golden hour with run and brisk walking alternately. First warm up by walking for a couple of minutes and then walk briskly. You can gradually increase your speed of brisk walking and running every few days. The idea is to exert enough to become breathless, sweat without much discomfort. In fact, you will enjoy it and feel like running more on holidays. You will be fit to compete in sports in a few weeks. While running, think how to improve your BMETR. If due to rain, you are unable to go outdoor, you can stand erect in one place and move your legs as if running (mock running) while standing on the same spot. You can complete the rest of programme indoor as well.

5 minutes: In *Shavasan,* lie flat on your back on a mat in a quiet airy room or verandah. Relax the whole body and keep your attention on the breath. Keep the limbs 1–2 ft apart with eyes closed. Keep the body still in a straight line. Run your attention to your body and limbs with calming effect. This asana helps you to get back your energy whenexhausted.

Second 20 Minutes: *Asana* and *Dhyana* combined.

Asana: It is meant to keep the body comfortable relaxed and stationary. In *Vajrasana,* kneel (fold your legs backwards) on your knees with soles of feet together facing backwards and upwards. Then lower your buttocks to rest on the heels and soles. Keep your head, neck and back (spine) straight and eyes closed. Hands should rest on your knees. Stay in this position and practice 20 minutes of *dhyana*at the same time. Thus, you sit still on heels like Mohammedans do while offering their prayers. *Sukhasana* is sitting cross-legged with right leg below the left thigh and left leg below the right thigh. You keep your spine and head and neck erect with eyes closed with hands on the knees.

Dhyana: While in *vajraasana* or *sukhasana,* keep your attention solely on your breath. You can feel the cold air entering through your nose during inhalation and warm air coming out through the nostrils when you breathe out. The air touches the upper part of your lips during exhalation. Keeping your attention on this movement of air (or any other object) without a break or noise is called *dhyana.* In *dhyana,* you keep attention on a single object. Please do not interfere or react to any thought which appears. Gradually the mind becomes calm and becomes one with the breath. Mind gradually gains the knack to focus on a single object or subject longer. A regular dhyana of just twenty minutes daily is the most important single activity for students. Your mental clarity and memory will improve and intelligence will get sharper. You will do better in studies or any other activity gradually.

It is easy to understand dhyana but is difficult to practise it. This is because mind (attention) is like a monkey and keeps jumping from one thing to the other. So, you have to get hold of your attention and observe the breath continuously coming in and out of your nostrils. Whenever your attention jumps to another object, bring it back to focusing your breath immediately and if necessary, do it repeatedly. The purpose of Dhyana is to keep the attention glued to the breath cycle (or on any other single entity) uninterruptedly for at least twenty minutes. If, due to some reasons, you run short of time to complete the the golden hour workout, then at least make room for dhyana in the morning. The rest of the session can be completed at any other time of the day. Mindfulness is keeping your attention limited to the present time and action in whatever you are doing. You can practice it during your waking hours. This has good effects similar to dhyana.

Mission Commitment

Third 20 Minutes: For exercise of mind, emotions and commitments.

Intelligence, attention and memory are already being exercised when you study, review or challenge the brain to solve problems. Discrimination is also exercised during the day long interactions.

So, we will now discuss about good and bad emotions which exist in all of us in variable proportion. We will commit to keep the bad emotions away from our thought, word and deed by practising the good emotions.

Is it not interesting to see innumerable emotions floating and fleeting at random in our thoughts? They are of various shades but can arguably be classified in two categories, good or constructive and bad or destructive depending on their effects on yourself and others. Let us examine the bad ones.

Basically there are three groups of bad emotions. Let us put them in three groups A,B and C. Group A and B, have four bad emotions in each. The group C has five in it. These emotions if not under control, can delay or spoil your chances of success in whatever you do. Their intensity increases if one encourages them.

Group A: Attracts like a magnet; they are: taking undue advantage from others, to be greedy, to steal and addiction to any harmful habit or substance e.g.alcohol, drugs.

Group B: Is nurturing illusion about yourself which may lead to- Arrogance, Hate, Anger and Violence.

Group C: Misleads us due to our ignorance: when we fail to see the reality of our or other's existence, worth and relationship. This creates, deception about them which is Maya, wrong notion of attachment Moha, causing Fear (Bhaya), Misery (Dukha).

Inertia (Lazynesss) is the last of the lot. It prevents you to achieve anything you wish to, by complacency or inaction. One who can comprehend its mischief can overpower all the bad emotions by being proactive in matters of your BMETR. This gives you an opportunity to turn a liability into an asset by decisive action. Bad emotions have limited but sometimes useful role to play. When someone bullies you, Ahankar in the form of self respect will give you the temper and strength to stop him. Parents use anger to discipline their erring wards. Please explore yourself to find some more. Think of how and where bad emotions are not bad after all.

One can be aware of each emotion by introspection of your past behaviour every morning, to correct them, and do your duty, without bias (Vivek). It will make you successful, happy and energetic.

Good or constructive emotions: These are difficult to practice in the beginning but will prove to be invaluable tools for your success. The good results may take time but will be solid and long lasting. They are Truth, Non-stealing (including examination), Non-violence, Compassion, Sacrifice (Sacrifice is when you forego a pleasant experience for a greater and good cause), Cleanliness, Helping the needy. These will be easy to practice if you take care of the aforesaid bad emotions. Your attitude and behaviour will then change you to be a good human being.

You will then not discriminate people on the basis of caste,colour creed, religion, sex or between the rich and the poor. You will be able to solve all personal problems yourself first before seeking help from others. You will try to forgive others' fault, will remain cheerful and respect the elders.Only management of emotions on a daily basis can create a rock solid foundation of your BMETR.

Write the above commitments about emotions and your ambition and dreams in an exclusive personal diary and read it daily. It is a saying that you can only change yourself and not others.

If for some reasons you are disappointed or can't concentrate on studies open this diary to reaffirm your faith on yourself and your ambitions.

Think about laziness. It could be physical, such as, unwillingness to go to a shop when it is necessary. It can be mental e.g., by postponing the study session and it can also be emotional, like when you do not say sorry or cheer up somebody, when you should. Please find out the Whys and Hows about the rest of the emotions by introspection.

All actions happen at the thought, speech or action level. They enter your thoughts first, and after processing, move to speech and finally to action level to give it a shape or substance. So, remain alert every day to watch your mind at these levels. After regular practice, it will lessen the conflicts and bad emotions and increase your energy and happiness.

Summary

There is no short cut to success

- Routine is the means to keep you steady on the path of your goal.
- Go through the study course, taking responsibility to understand and remember it.
- Coaching and tuition are a form of guidance and encouragement. They cannot help unless your own first hand basic preparation of a subject is solid.

- Adolescence is a period of growth of BME which is ideal time to improve your brain power and learning.

- Time cares for no one and so it is up to you to extract the maximum advantage out of it. If the day seems to be packed with distractions, somehow complete your study task first.

- School is the ideal place to learn and grow as a person.

- That golden hour of 60 minutes in early morning is the period to ensure golden habits for lifelong achievements. Please don't ever miss it even for a day.

- If due to some reasons you cannot go to a playing field for games, then do physical exercise, yoga and dhyana indoor.

- Listen to music or enjoy indoor games like ludo or chess for entertainment.

- When you feel out of sorts, visit a place of natural beauty like park, river or ocean to relax and recharge. It will normalise and rejuvenate you.

- Some good habits are to drink half to one liter of water in empty stomach after getting up from bed.

- Brushing with neem twig (or some other suitable twigs) is good for teeth and gums. Press your jaws tight in toilet to make them strong. Brushing teeth is followed by cleaning the tongue with a Tongue scraper in the morningand brushing the teeth before going to bed is a good habit.

- Wash your hands, including wrist, first thing in the morning or after coming home from outside and at all other times before meals. Wash your mouth after you had meals, snacks or a drink other than water. Cut your nails regularly.

- Neti or water cleansing of nose is helpful in upper respiratory tract problems. It is recommended in air pollution or chronic upper respiratory tract problems. It is a 10-minutes procedure in early morning. It can be learnt from a yoga teacher.

- Vitamin D is important for bones (growth, teeth, etc.) and many other important functions of the body. Many Indians suffer from deficiency of this important vitamin. A weekly 30-minutes' exposure to sun between 10 AM to 3 PM will be adequate.

- Read the daily routine regularly till it is a habit. Read one chapter of this book once a week.

- Routine is like music set in a frame of lyrics, rhythm and tune. The lyrics or narrative may change with your age but let the tune and rhythm continue lifelong.

Mind Map 8: A ROUTINE FOR LIFE

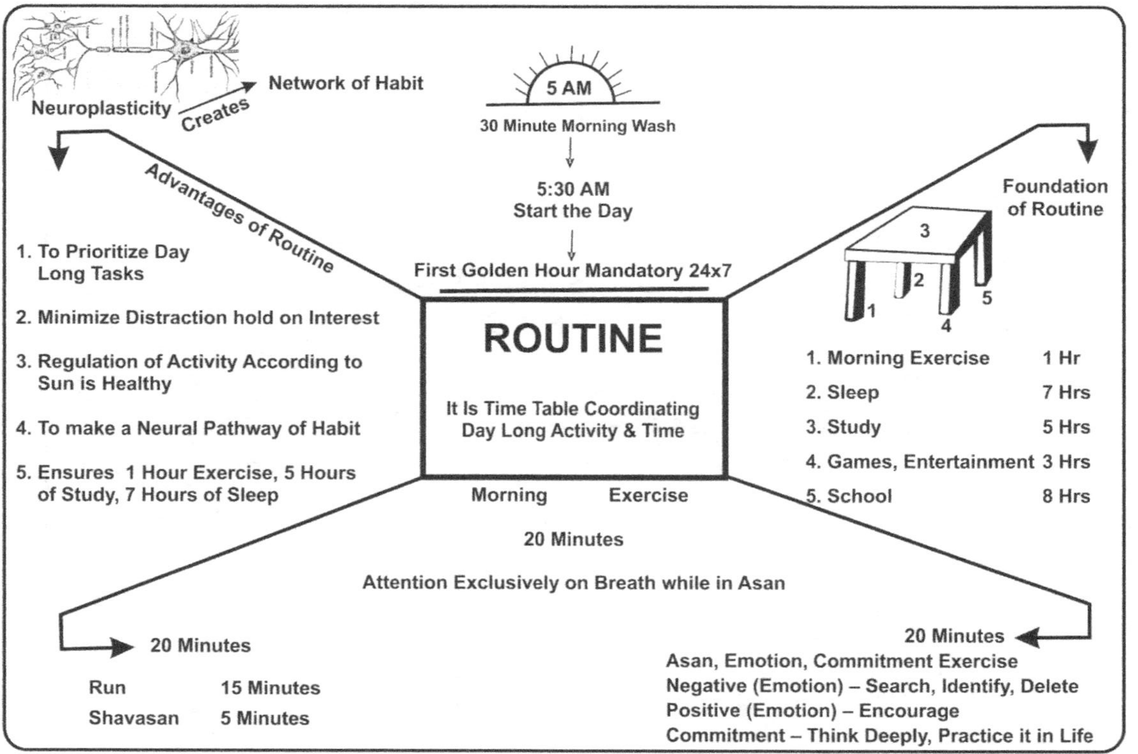

Mind Map 9: THE DIFFERENT ASANAS

References

Buzan, Barry and Tony. 1996. *The Mind Map Book.*UK: Educational Publishers LLP trading BBC.

Carver K., Joyner K., and Udry J.R. (2003). 'National Estimates of Adolescent Romantic Relationships'. *Adolescent Romantic Relationships and Sexual Behavior: Theory, Research, and Practical Implications*, 291–329.

Darren, E.R. and Warburton, Crystal Whitney Nicol. 2006. 'Health Benefits of Physical Activity: The Evidence, C.M.R.J.',174(6): 801–09.

Dumont, Theron Q. 2011. *The Power of Concentration.* US: Good Books Distribution Publication (1st edition 1991).

Fabrega, Marelisa. 2018. 'Fourteen Ways to Increase YourIQ'. Available on: https://daringtolivefully.com/increase-your-iq (accessed on 26 April 2020).

Fernandez, Alvaro and Elkhonon Goldberg. 2009. *The Sharp Brains Guide to Brain Fitness.* (Second Edition with Pascale Michelon Sharp Brains, Inc; 2013).

Foer, Joshua. 2011. *Moon Walking with Einstein.*New York: Penguin Books.

Gardner, H. 1983. 'Frames of Mind'. *The Theory of Multiple Intelligences.* NewYork: Basic Books.

Goenka, S.N. 2014. Ten Day Vippasana Meditation Course.Taught by S.N. Goenka. Available on: http://gurmeet.net/spiritual/vipassana-meditation-taught-by-s-n-goenka-partii/ (accessed on 21 April 2020).

Harsha, David W., and Gerald S. Berenson. 1995. 'The Benefits of Physical Activity in Childhood'. Available on: https://www.sciencedirect.com/science/article/abs/pii/S000296291534979X (accessed on 26 April 2020).

Kawashima,Ryuta. 2014.*Train Your Brain*. Bhopal: Manjul Publishing House.

Krishnamurti, J. 1999. *The Revolution from within*. California: Krishnamurti Foundation of America.

Legge, Armi. 2015. 'The Compelling Science behind Early Morning Starts'. Available on: https://completehumanperformance.com/2015/09/11/early-morning-starts/(accessed on 26 April 2020).

M.D., Shahid Ali. 2011. 'Early Detection of Illicit Drug Use in Teenagers'. *Innov. Clin. Neurosci*, 8(12): 24–28.

Morris J N, and JA Heady and PPB Raffle and CG Roberts and JN Parks and Lancet. 1953.'Coronary Heart Disease and Physical Activity of Work',2:1053–57.

Paul, Kevin. 1999.*Study Smarter, Not Harder* (17th edition, 2013). Mumbai: Jaico Publishing House.

Rider. 1991. 'The Miracle of Mindfulness'. *Thich Nhat Hahn*. London: Ebury Publishing, imprint of Penguin Random House.

Saraswati, Swami Satyananda. 2004. *AsanPranayam Mudra Bandh*.Munger: Yoga Publication Trusy.

Sobesky, J.L.2014.'High Fat Diet Consumption Disrupts Memory and Brain Behav Immune'. Colorado: University of Colorado, 42,22–32.

Strong, William B et al. 2005. 'Evidence Based Physical Activityfor School-Age Youth'.*The Journal of Pediatrics*, 146(6): 732–37.

Tanner, J. 1972. 'Sequence, Tempo, and Individual Variation in Growth and Development of Boys and Girls Aged Twelve to Sixteen'. In *Twelve to Sixteen: Early Adolescence*, edited by J. Kagan and R. Coles. New York: Norton.

Vadakayil, Ajit. 2014. 'Shravan Manan and Nididhyasan'. Available at: http://ajitvadakayil.blogspot.com/ (accessed on 26 April 2020).

Walton, Alice G. 2015. '7 Ways Meditation Can Actually Change the Brain'. Available at: https://www.forbes.com/sites/alicegwalton/2015/02/09/7-ways-meditation-can-actually-change-the-brain/#2e24f9441465 (Last accessed on 21 April 2020).

Wikipedia. 2008. 'Adolescence'. Available on: https://en.wikipedia.org/wiki/Adolescence(accessed on 26 April 2020).

Woodyard, Catherine. 2011. 'Exploring the Therapeutic Effects of Yogaand Its Ability to Increase Quality of Life'. *International Journal of Yoga*, Jul–Dec, 4(2): 49–54.

Wujec, Tom. 2008. *The Complete Mental Fitness Book*. New Delhi: Orient Paperbacks.

7Habits That May Actually Change The Brain According to Science www.wellnesssrocks.com au.

http://wellnessrocks.com.au/7-habits-that-may-actually-change-the-brain-according-to-science/ Last accessed on May2.2020.

www.ingramcontent.com/pod-product-compliance
Lightning Source LLC
LaVergne TN
LVHW010017200726
843495LV00015B/1810